Finishing the Picture

Ian Abbot (1947-1989)

For Frances Abbot

Acknowledgements

The editor would like to thank Frances Abbot, Joy Hendry, Alexander Hutchison, Hilary Kundu and Tessa Ransford for their support, help and contributions to this collection.

Thanks must also go to the staff of the National Library of Scotland, the Scottish Poetry Library, and the special collections departments of Glasgow University Library and Edinburgh University Library.

Contents

Acknowledgements	*vii*
'Torn into being': Ian Abbot and his Poems	
by Tessa Ransford	*xv*
Foreword by Alexander Hutchison	*xix*
Introduction	*xxv*

Avoiding the Gods — 1

Ferns like poems	2
Forms	3
The bestiary of Cortes	4
Montezuma	5
Vestal	6
Crossing the ford	7
Inside the altarpiece	8
Spoor	10
Ariel	11
Marriages	12
Scott's first voyage	13
The last entry of a polar explorer	16
A crofter buried	17
A body of work	18
Caliban rising	19
Ewe against the fence	21
Avoiding the gods	23
Before the flood	24
The suicides of April	25
An inland sea	26

I – The astrologer	27
II – The knight	28
III – The Queen	29
Shrapnel	30
One place in the Highlands	31
Landscape of a Highland gentleman	32
Tick	33
The beetle man	34
Promenaders on the tideline	35
Digging for victory	36
Hephaestus preaching	37
Ward seven – December	39
Exile	40
A cancelled poetry lesson	41
Drawing to a close	42
Blizzard conditions	43
The oriental archer	44
Agates	45
Quiet evenings at home	46
The sailor's widow embroidering	47
Death watch	48
Lament of the horse-bit	49
Laurel bush	50
A search for lodgings	51
Fishing through a hole	52
Sloughing	54
Fever	55
Wax resist	56
Last dip of the year	57
A vanished poet's house	58
Lifeline	60
Monster	61
The shadow-wolf	62
Ga-Cridhe	63
Crossing Carn Donnachaidh	64
Bird's eye view	65
Brain coral	66

A late note from a prodigal	67
Rites of passage	68
A late note to my mother	70
The mechanisms of the gin	71
Drifts	72
A woman of my acquaintance	73
Finishing the picture	74
Drowning among mountains	75
Uninvited guests	76
Black name	77
Chalybeate spring	78
Harbingers	79
A memoir from the mind-camp	80

Poems published in magazines but not included in *Avoiding the Gods* — 81

Here	82
How important	84
The mine	85
Departures	86
On that day	87
Small hours	90
A resurrected long dead soldier	91
Stalactites	92
Love in February	93
November	94
Spring Equinox	95
Moths at the window	96
Looking with new eyes	97
Keeper and cottage	98
The comforting word	99
Climbing through ammonites	100
A mad old woman dying	101
Speaking in solitary	102
Passing through September	103
Life history	104
Looking for wild men	105

Poems first published posthumously   **107**
An educated rabbit's view of the snare   108
Cameraman   109
On certain nights   110
Musteline   111
A real death   112
The poetry of television   113
Landscapes   114
The omnibus   115
Starlings   116
A summer engagement   117
How I forgot   118
Throughout the green night   119
He caught me by the roadside   120

Unpublished poems   **121**
I seem   122
To Hilary   125
After the Equinox   126
Raptor   127
White hands, slender   128
The retired soldier's lesson   129
Tumour   131
Omens   133
Khamsin   134
Mykonos   135
A.M. alphabet   136
Evening   137
Plain of jars   138
Returning   139
The magi in solitude   141
Prayer to the god of the mine   142
Thoughts after the funeral, for W.   143
Dreams in the evening   144
Writing late   145
Retrospective premonitions   146

Unpublished notebook or draft poems	**147**
Along the wall the heads look down	148
Within me	149
River of deep winter, when the ice	150
Here is where	151
History rolls away	152
I know that somewhere	153
Three words, no more	154
Here in September	155
Death in the rose	158
You will say	159
Trees	160
The wind blows	161
In my veins the pack is running	162
Notes	*165*
Select Bibliography	*169*
Index of First Lines	*175*

'Torn into being': Ian Abbot and his Poems

Ian Abbot's poems first came to my attention in the seventies and eighties, when he was a regular subscriber to *Lines Review* poetry magazine and a supporter of the Scottish Poetry Library – inspirationally visiting schools in the North East with our van tours for instance – and I thought of him as a poet who confronted the relentless indifference of nature to humankind but who found here and there a symbolic or particular significance. His was no happy, comforting, entertaining poetry, but a poetry unflinchingly seeking its own truth however ominous. Indeed an otherwordly sense of presences, around and within us asking to be heard and allowed their say, hovers within and over the poems.

Ian was encouraged by poet, writer and editor, William Montgomerie when in Dundee and it was during Montgomerie's editorship of *Lines Review* (1977-82) that he first began to appear regularly. In those days, poets were often published in magazines for decades before venturing on a collection. Ian's first collection, *Avoiding the Gods*, came out from Chapman Publishing in 1988 after such an interval. That he died a year later was tragic for Scottish literature — his death almost on a par with Camus in significance for Scotland I would claim.

This is not because of any particular poem, though there are many I value, but because of the body of his work and its Rilke-like preoccupation with the processes of poetry in body and mind. Nature was for him not a concept of the world systems in which he lived, but of the systems which lived in him. His was a life devoted to poetry, as Rilke's was. That does not mean devoted to being successful or published, but devoted to the life which is demanded by those processes at whatever cost in terms of comfort or relationships.

In his work, Ian trains himself to hear 'the voice' of the abandoned horse-bit found in the soil ('Lament of the horse-bit'), or the voice of the spear ('Ga-Cridhe'), and requires himself to even shut the door on his own voice ('A search for lodgings'). Much of this listening and experimenting and waiting concerns language itself (perhaps comparable to the approach of W. S. Graham in this respect) and several poems liken language to aspects of nature. For instance, 'The language lies in the road like stones' ('Agates'); the 'Ariel' and 'Caliban' stories in *The Tempest*; raising 'the long rifle of language to my shoulder' ('Spoor'); 'the words/that wait to blossom at my fingers' ends' ('Crossing the Ford'); 'transparency of leaves is in my speech' and 'my language is a deer dismembered under pines' ('A body of work').

Metaphors of fishing are used, and of snares. Joy and terror cannot be separated. The retriever dogs are 'dazzling harbingers of a day of blood' ('Harbingers'). Sillions are joyful – perhaps unconsciously borrowed from Hopkins – but 'the purity of snow/is terrible'. He is a linnet singing in the 'interminable dark' ('Bird's eye view'); while the making of a poem is like the dying of a stag seen through binoculars ('Finishing the picture').

The ways of predators, that allow 'numberless small deaths' and the vicious contraptions of the gods: crosses, iron wings, armies...('Avoiding the gods'); the ignorant evil of sheep in the Highlands; and even 'the rising murderous rapture of the Spring' disturb him in his physical as well as mental being and extract the poems from him. He compares the poetic process to the life-cycle of the tick, and, most gruesome perhaps of all, he describes a poem as 'torn into being' ('Raptor'). All in all, there is no resolution, as he concludes in 'A crofter buried': 'In time the earth accepts from you/the price of everything you borrowed from it.'

I welcome this new collection and this chance for Abbot to be recognised at a time when poetry in Scotland is in danger of becoming perhaps too much like clever comment. If Rilke were to come among us, he would be at one with Ian Abbot in his harsh Highland home.

Tessa Ransford

Foreword

Ian Abbot's sudden death in 1989 called back one of the best poets writing in Scotland at the time. I had only known him for a few years, but I was sure of his worth, his authority, the strength and range of his imagination, his consistent and skilful deployment of words.

I first met him when Joy Hendry paired us to read upstairs at Ryrie's Bar in the Haymarket during the Edinburgh Festival in 1985. I'm not sure why exactly, but we were scheduled to read from 7.30 to closing time – which was then roughly 11.00 o'clock. Even with Josephine (Jo) Miller also there to provide songs and give us music on the fiddle it looked like being a long haul. As it turned out, just about everybody had a good time, bobbing along on various enthusiasms; but for me meeting Jo and Ian was a pleasure that lasted.

Ian's reading manner was clear and deliberate, the voice setting out the measure of each poem so you sensed the shape as the theme was advanced. It appeared both formal and organic somehow, and he very rarely mis-stepped or fluffed a line. "This guy is *good*," I said to myself, and looked a bit more carefully at the sheaf of poems in my lap.

Toward the end of the evening (not out of material, but running a little thin) I cranked up and sang: getting through Patrick Kavanagh's 'Raglan Road' after a couple of false starts. When I sat down Ian leaned over and said in my ear: "If I'd known you were going to sing, I would have brought my moothie". The impression I got that night of someone easy and convivial, but with a meticulous and proper sense of his art, was confirmed for me as we got to know each other better.

Ian had courage, and no false airs or graces. That much at least of his character you can connect to the fabric and content of his poems. The work is not narrowly Scottish, although it can engage local or national issues with power and immediacy. The language is rich and beautifully phrased; the tone is both personal and measured. Dismissing the agents of a predatory, supernatural world, refusing echoes of old liturgy, he says:

> Let us remain here, calmly
> taking bread, and wine, and speech.
> and in the morning
> take our limbs to work, and walk behind
> the swaying, fuming breath of cattle.
>
> And let us look for our salvation
> in the language we have come to teach ourselves.

Ian was too hard-headed to over-simplify; and he didn't aspire to mere rusticity. His poem 'Ewe against the Fence' is a corrective against any drift to plausible romanticism, as is the conclusion of 'A Crofter Buried':

> You thought to print the earth indelibly.
> But now let down, and burdened
> with the bare field's sullen weight,
> you must lie still and be content.
> the cairn begins to crumble
> even as the final stone is being placed.
>
> Your footprints are already blowing shut.
> In time the earth accepts from you
> the price of everything you borrowed from it.

What the poet has to say at each stage is contained by the elegance and clarity of his forms, even in poems as dark as 'Ga-Cridhe,' or when, before the guns, the 'lean, red dogs' picking up the scent are

> floated forward, almost motionless;
> the dazzling harbingers of a day of blood.

In one of the published but previously uncollected pieces printed here, 'Climbing through ammonites', there is evidence of how Abbot can join themes of close, even intimate, connection with the true scope of existence. It is one of the things that gives his poems 'authority' – a term I chose earlier. He doesn't overstretch himself, the language is fitting, unpretentious, even when it includes 'very soul' and 'eternal'; yet all of it conveys the huge chasms that lie on either side of any life, while at the same time offering a wish – not quite a prayer, and not anything to command – for something to share within that space, within the possibilities that extend to 'you and I'.

Once at a literary gathering in Edinburgh I was trying, without success, to check on the origin of the word 'auspices'. I knew it had to do with divination, but couldn't remember how, and all the suggestions I got were haphazard or facetious. Finally I pounced on Ian and put the question again. "It's about birds," he said, "– interpreting the pattern of their flight". I recognized straightaway that he was right. And I dug up the bit from Spenser: 'Time ... taught me the sooth of birds by beating of their wings'. Well, we must have thought for a little while we were the only 'boogers' there (as Hamish Henderson would probably have it) who knew what was what.

Since he died I've kept looking to the patterns, and often he comes to mind: the crows on top of Salisbury Crags in Edinburgh, spinning and dipping in the thermals; or down on the tarmac a chirm of starlings headed for crumbs. A while ago now, on a drive up to Cairnpapple Hill I saw a single magpie flap from a branch, and it took some time looking round to make up the pair. Sorrow and joy are not so pat in Ian's poems, nor in the thoughts of his friends; but I don't expect one without the balance of the other.

I've made two poems for Ian Abbot since his death: 'The Holt' and 'The Hat'. Both are short, and both quite different from each other. In the first I tried to convey his natural mystery, his brilliance, his dark recesses and clear lines; in the second, his strong affection and vitality.

The Holt
(for Ian)

sinuous
from shadow

unsheathed
and silver

no pounce-work
no grudge-music

words are in
the breathing ground

this uncircum-
scribable air

The Hat

I thought I saw you.
I thought I could see you
come in and wander round –
I thought I recognised the hat.

Wherever it is you've clambered
off to, is there anyone there
to twist a story, lift a dram?

I could have sworn it was you –
my hand is out - even now I'm
smiling, waiting to say hullo.

    I trust this book comes at the right time, and will help to reinforce what Ian Abbot did so well. Certainly the opportunity is here to make a better acquaintance with this fine poet and the astonishing world he chose to shape and echo.

Alexander Hutchison

    [This recollection makes use of material in 'Remembering Ian Abbot' published in *Chapman* magazine in 2003]

Introduction

It is now over a quarter of a century since the publication of Ian Abbot's first and only collection *Avoiding the Gods* by Chapman Publishing in 1988. There were to be no subsequent collections during Abbot's lifetime because a year later, Abbot was killed in a car crash close to his home in Whitebridge, near Inverness when his Ford Fiesta careered off the road at around 7pm in the evening on 18th October, 1989. Joy Hendry, editor of *Chapman* and Abbot's publisher, remarked that he was 'killed in a car crash on his way home from being a pall-bearer at the funeral of a young local boy who had also been killed in a crash on that same road, the B852'.[1] The coincidence seems so grim as to almost be the work of fiction, but in the *Scotsman* account of his death, the reporter hinted that Abbot had been working on a follow-up collection of poems to *Avoiding the Gods*.

In 2003, Abbot's friend and fellow poet Alexander Hutchison called for a 'new edition of his work, and a broader appreciation of his worth'.[2] The poems that comprise this present volume are the complete text of *Avoiding the Gods* plus poems in various stages of finish and publication. In Abbot's archives in the National Library of Scotland, deposited by his widow Frances in 2007, there is no clear indication of plans for a second collection, although there is easily enough material for such a collection, scattered across 13 folders. However, it is clear that Abbot sought to retain drafts of his poems, to show how meticulously they were produced, from initial pencil sketches to poems hammered out on typewriter and annotated in pen. Often the paper Abbot used was that of his own silversmithing company 'Abbot Silver', which ran aground because of the vagaries of the tourist trade and the soaring prices of precious metals, or the letter-headed paper of other companies which had employed him to do various manual jobs.

What emerges from all these papers, is that writing and poetry became central to Abbot's identity and one of the primary reasons why he took some hard and dangerous jobs, several of which informed his poems. For instance, a job as a fence-erector gave him the inspiration for 'Scott's first voyage' when Abbot imagined getting caught in a snowdrift on the hill on which he was working at the time. The thought of being trapped by snow made him think of the explorations of Captain Scott. Abbot, as someone who worked outdoors often, saw avoiding harsh weather as akin to mastering a form of language from the landscape, of being able to communicate with it to preclude disaster:

> And that dumb voice drifts still
> into the small bones of my ears
> as under me I feel
> my own slow glacier begin to stir
> and carry me away.
> Embedded like a rock I go
> to score myself
> along the deep trench of the world; at last to scratch
> my little history into the bitter landscape waiting.

This present volume also contains poems that were published by Abbot during his lifetime, but uncollected into book form, ranging from his first appearance in San Franciscan counter-culture arts journal *Kayak* in 1968 to a long standing relationship with *Lines Review* which began with Abbot's old tutor, William Montgomerie, taking up the position as editor and passing on to subsequent editors a high regard for Abbot's poems. Writing about Abbot in a blurb for the back cover of *Avoiding the Gods,*

Montgomerie was to describe him as a 'brilliant student' who produced poems like hatching 'butterflies'. Speaking of teaching Abbot in the 1960s, Montgomerie recalled that 'as I gave my lectures on English literature, I was really addressing Ian Abbot, sitting exactly in the centre of the front row of students'.[3] Montgomerie would eventually consider Abbot to have been 'one of the very best poets I knew ... I had a very high estimate of Ian's importance as a man, and as a poet'.[4]

There are also poems here that are to be found carefully typed and preserved that were destined for publication but never made it to that stage, and there are poems that appear as drafts, handwritten in notebooks. Abbot's archive also contains a great number of short stories that are in their own right often full of literary merit. However, the concern with this volume is Abbot's poems and while this is a collection of some of his best and most representative material, it is not a complete collection, but rather an edited gathering of those available works it seemed appropriate to publish at this time.

The aim of this book, then, is twofold: to address the abrupt end of Abbot's poetry and to attempt to secure his reputation as a poet. Despite his poem 'The mechanisms of the gin' being anthologised by Douglas Dunn for his Faber and Faber *Twentieth Century Scottish Poetry,* Abbot's poems have only briefly appeared in print since his death, in a retrospective in 2003 by *Chapman* and a handful of poems appearing in *Northwords Now* and *The Dark Horse*.

In his memoir of the poet in *Chapman* 102-103 (2003), Alexander Hutchison wrote: 'When *Avoiding the Gods* was published by Chapman I remember being disappointed by the reception it got in some quarters, since the poems were clearly as good as anything else appearing at the time'.[5] Hutchison did, however, also note that Abbot and his poetry had not lacked champions; and this was true before and after Abbot's death. William Montgomerie had certainly promoted the work through *Lines Review*; Tessa Ransford secured him readings and workshops through the Scottish Poetry Library in the late 1980s, and Joy Hendry's faith in his work and regard for its quality was evident in her publication and promotion of *Avoiding the Gods* in 1989.

Among other admirers and supporters impressed by the power of the poems were the writers James and Janet Caird, then living in Inverness, who became friends and correspondents with Abbot – and James Caird's death is observed in the same *Scottish Poetry Library Newsletter* as Abbot's. Significantly, in 1992, Colin Nicholson devoted a chapter of his book *Poem, Purpose and Place: Shaping Identity in Contemporary Scottish Verse* to Abbot's work and a conversation he had with the poet about his writing practices. Abbot's poems were also included, for example, in *Scottish Literature in the Twentieth Century*, edited by David McCordick (2002).

However, it is worth briefly revisiting what was expounded in contemporary reviews of *Avoiding the Gods*. Tony McManus, in *Cencrastus,* asserts that reading Abbot's poems amounts to seeing the landscape 'through a curtain of persistent rain, turning everything to greyness, a depressing dullness' and that Abbot speaks 'continually of death [...] the effect is positively dispiriting'.[6] In a tellingly anonymous review in *The Edinburgh Review* Abbot's poetry is condemned with tepid praise: 'a certain inarticulate charm, precisely because the author believes himself to be supremely knowing. Abbot's high mystical style succeeds because, in falling so completely short of its objectives, it shows us a man so pure in heart he thinks he can digress on Ariel and Caliban as if for the first time. The poems suggest an author who is attracted by the idea of being a poet; someone who thinks that blessed state is an end in itself.'[7] The tone of the review is imperious and inkhorn, almost as if an undergraduate in English Literature at the time was out to make a name for themselves as a trenchant reviewer, even though the piece is anonymous. The concept of a poem having a cynically emotive design on a reader, having 'objectives', is far removed from any experience I have had from reading Abbot's poems. It is true that Abbot talks at length about death, his landscapes are harsh and there is sometimes a vatic otherworldliness to the writing that might risk sounding portentous, but then I could single out these qualities in numerous other Scottish poets of the 20th century. Perhaps the most untenable view expounded here is that, because a literary character has been written about before and authoritatively, poets should steer clear from it in the future, such as Ariel. Surely one of the most important functions a poem can perform is a re-wiring or re-working, of established ways of thinking about entrenched narratives.

Both reviewers also put about the mistaken claim that Abbot's poems are serious and about death to the point of being depressing. While there are many poems in *Avoiding the Gods* that were written in earnest, there are equally others that show a more playful or celebratory side to Abbot's craft. In 'Last dip of the Year', the poem about which *The Herald* said Abbot took the subject's identity to his grave, he witnesses a young woman preparing to go swimming in a river.[8] The image we get of this woman is one couched in the natural world, with a 'body shy as berries', 'stepping neatly as a hind' out of the bush where she had undressed. There is more happening here than merely a vignette of a naked woman bathing, caught in the male gaze. She is casting off the clothes of a material world and finds herself going back into nature, caught on the cusp of a significant rite of passage, of imminent motherhood, but even here danger is entwined with beauty:

> Her tiny, berry-crimson breasts flared out
> like signals from the cool depths, warning
> of another season's turning and the spates to come.

There is a baptismal quality to these poems, a shrugging off of the old to embrace the cold winds that blast through their woods and sentences, the ego of the mortal poet grappling with things that are almost beyond the reach of even his finely tuned linguistic and poetic capacities. For all of the grave dignity that these poems carry, Abbot does not want us to despair, for the poem that can make you feel any emotion is written in the language of salvation, of earth and education. In terms of education, we also see a display of Abbot's dry wit in the poem 'A cancelled poetry lesson', where the poet, working from home as a private creative writing tutor, mixes both the standard teacher/pupil letter with an in-depth look at the precarious nature of writing and inspiration:

> There are some days
> when great clouds build up in the mind [...]
>
> On other days I might have sent
> my wicked, private terriers tunnelling
> to flush them out [...]
>
> So do not send
> your little girl today. Tomorrow may be better,
> but my prognosis for this afternoon is bad.

Colin Nicholson predicted that Abbot's poem 'Avoiding the gods' would become the title of his first collection, for speaking 'to the strengths in human self-sufficiency which Abbot's writing promotes'. By listening to 'the muscular cadences of his own writing' we as readers find a 'kind of release'.[9] Alexander Hutchison says in his Foreword, that 'sorrow and joy are not so pat in Ian's poems', but there can be a celebratory aspect in Abbot's work, exemplified in poems such as 'The omnibus':

> The street was wide
> and crowded with round faces,
> it was the morning a war had ended
> and if I'd a hat
> I'd have tossed it high
> into the brightening air.

However, more often, Abbot is a poet of landscapes and wildernesses which are 'sublime' in the original sense of the word, as places that inspire fear, wonder and inspiration. Abbot's view of poetry and language is intimately connected to that land and humanity's often bootless attempts to manage, abuse, change or profit from it. Colin Nicholson reminds us that Abbot was 'urban' by birth, his move to Whitebridge in 1974 'amounted, almost, to learning a new language, acquiring, in his words "the voices of the various kinds of landscape"'.[10] Consider, for instance, the alternate narratives explored in 'The mechanisms of the gin' between the hunting family who sets the traps and what the trap says when it is left to its own devices in the woods:

You tend it with utmost care. Intimately prime as your father did
its double jagged sickles and its tight-sprung mouth, arrange
its hidden ribbon of links. Then turn for home, moving
heavily downward into sleep.
Only to dream of iron laughter shouting in the wood
and the spare, insatiable gaze
that will see your own flesh folded in the earth
and then will sit back patient, waiting;
grinning till the wandered, bone-white stars begin to fall.

Often, Abbot sees landscape in a meta-poetic way, that is to say that all of the processes of expression and creativity are reflected in the new things and experiences that he has in a rural landscape. Ferns become like poems:

[...] I warn you

to approach them with respect.
Carelessly fingered, every covering stem
will strip you to the bone;
lay your soft hands open.
And innocently celebrate the spilling of your blood.

Abbot also sees the agates that he finds lying in the road like a form of language. Any passer-by can kick them away, the poet's task is to:

> Only pick it up and split it, polish it
> over and again
> with dust and finer dust and patience,
> and hold it up at length against the light.
>
> Then you will find its unseen, echoing rings.
> Then you will see how its limitless rainbows
> irradiate the world, your substance, and your ordinary skin.

One of the recurrent themes in Abbot's work is that of being hunted, of a life-or-death chase or quest, which Abbot views as an aesthetic, intellectual and existential one. Abbot wrote that people leave spoors, and by these they will inevitably be hunted down and that the ultimate 'body of work' is how the earth moves to inhabit us once and for all, after death. It is by a slow process of piecing things together that I have been able to get a clear picture of Abbot and the scope of his work. In 'Spoor' Abbot writes that:

> And one day I will catch him on the skyline,
> relaxed and unaware, until I raise
> the long rifle of language to my shoulder
> and hold my breath, and squeeze
> and squeeze.
> And watch the words like bullets home in for the kill,
> and hear
> the echoes roll away around the world.

Reflected in this, we can see Abbot aware of the fact that he was as much the hunter as the hunted. At the same time there is a consistent impulse through the work to establish identity, to leave evidence of it, and of seeking ways to prevent its erasure – a threat of obliteration described most vividly in 'A crofter buried' where, following the poor man's death, we learn even his 'footprints are already blowing shut.'

Part of the impetus here is to ensure that there is less risk of things 'blowing shut' on Ian Abbot's work, since there are few enough points of access as things stand. It is only available in the original Chapman first edition, of which Tony McManus, writing his review in 1988 said that the book was already falling apart due to poor binding.[11] A few more poems were published in Chapman's 1999 'Memorial Special Edition' of *Avoiding the Gods*.[12] Both are hard to find and both are particularly fragile productions.

As much as Abbot's work was admired and followed by certain members of the Scottish literary community, he often struggled to secure the publication of his work. While Abbot wrote and published since the 1960s, the 1980s was truly his peak in terms of output in magazines, yet with the exception of a handful of published poems, almost all appeared in *Lines Review* beginning under William Montgomerie's editorship. Abbot's archive shows us that he preserved a great number of his rejection slips, thus giving us a sense of the scale of opposition Abbot faced as a poet, and his ceaseless dedication to his work. In 'The Holt' by Alexander Hutchison (printed in the Foreword) we see Abbot being compared to an otter with its dark, sleek, predatory, amphibious qualities. His 'wild' character is part of his mystery. In the same poem the references to 'no pounce work/no grudge-music' suggest his directness, his lack of embellishment as mere decoration, and his removal from the usual contemporary scenes without embitterment – lifted (as the last lines convey) to an element evading easy definition, above mere fad or fashion.

Not much interview material survives of Abbot's, apart from Colin Nicholson's essay-cum-interview 'A Kind of Logic' which has been referred to in this book for explanatory notes to certain poems. We do not know, for instance, poets he cited as influences, although there are poems by Dylan Thomas, Iain Crichton Smith, T. S. Eliot, Norman Nicholson, Tagore and Blake hand-written by Abbot amongst his papers. He was not an introverted and reclusive poet, but an active member of the School of Poets, editing in 1985 their annual calendar of poems written by members. He also, as Tessa Ransford reminds us, regularly gave readings with fellow poets from Harvey Holton to Sorley MacLean and poetry workshops, particularly in schools. For his television appearance, on *In Verse* for STV in the late 1980s, he read for ten minutes and the poems he chose were 'The mechanisms of the gin', 'Ariel', 'Ewe against the fence' (which he claimed was based on the Clearances) and 'Drowning among mountains'. Given that he died so shortly afterwards, it seems reasonable to conjecture that these were some of his current favourite poems, or ones he felt the strongest, all coming as he claimed from real life occurrences and experiences.

Thanks again to Colin Nicholson's research and interest in Abbot in the late 1980s and Abbot's own self-penned biographical statement in *Avoiding the Gods*, we can begin to piece together his life and times. Born Ian Robert Hamilton Abbot in Perth in 1947, he was to list 1944 and 1945 as his date of birth in order to sound more senior in his applications and submissions. He was the son of a house-painter and grew up in a 'bleak tenement' on Ruthven Avenue in the city and he attended the Northern District School. His family then moved to Rannoch Road and Abbot went to Goodlyburn Primary School. He left Perth Academy at the age of 15 to work in the Tay Salmon Fisheries where he became increasingly active in left-wing politics. Of his youthful political engagement, Abbot writes in Nicholson's unpublished notes:

> I think you owe it to yourself to undermine as far as possible the things that people are trying to make you think, trying to make you feel; things you're expected to think and feel simply because you're in a certain level of society or belong to a particular stratum.[13]

In the 1960s, Abbot went to Dundee Commercial College to obtain the Highers he missed at school. Here he met the poet William Montgomerie, whose classes Abbot attended. These classes and Montgomerie's support ignited Abbot's interest in poetry. After college, Abbot found work as a psychiatric nurse at the Royal Edinburgh Hospital where he also worked in a 'geriatric ward'. From there he entered the University of Edinburgh's Medical Faculty and later transferred to the University of Stirling for a psychology degree – which he never completed, having lost his interest in academia. In the early 1970s he entered into business as a silversmith and moved to his final home in Whitebridge, which he would often facetiously refer to as being 'on the wrong side of Loch Ness'.[14] Abbot went even further to describe Whitebridge as 'a loose collection of houses in the hills above Loch Ness [...] about one third the size of what would generally be referred to as a hamlet'.[15] Owing to the smallness and remoteness of this near 'hamlet' his silversmith business dried up. From this point on he worked at a succession of precarious and casual farm jobs such as 'sheep-clipping, fence erection, tractor driving, pony work' and his biographical statement in *Avoiding the Gods* claims he also worked as an auditor, a lorry and bus driver, an interior designer, a woodcutter, a barman, a civil servant, a builder's labourer. In his application for a Scottish Arts Council bursary, he claimed that he often worked these jobs to 'finance travels through Europe and Africa' but that his ultimate aim was to become a 'full-time and self-supporting writer'. In letters to William Montgomerie, Abbot confessed that there were also delaying tactics to his various jobs, to put off the scary thought of risking everything with writing.[16] His chequered employment experience was not without note, as Alexander Hutchison reminds us in an anecdote:

> Ian was driving down from Inverness with two hefty companions to pick up sheep at the Perth sales. When the sheep were stowed, and the pubs were dry, they set off

North, with the sober Abbot driving. The two side-kicks fell asleep, and soon were jolting heavily together in the narrow cab as the lorry took the twisty road home. After a while Ian got fed up of being banged around by these two big snoring lummoxes, and stopped to sort it out. In a trice, the comatose *compadres* were roped together and lashed up snug to the off-side door. Sanguine, satisfied, free of encumbrances, Ian climbed back in behind the wheel.

A few miles later, who should it be but the boys in blue come flashing up to pull the lorry over. They were looking for sheep-rustlers, or so they said, and they quizzed Ian close, checked over the papers from the sale, and made a quick tally of the woolly cargo bleating in the back. Before they left, one of the bobbies shone his torch around the cab, revealing for the first time Pinky and Perky, still trussed up and still oblivious. "I'm not even going to comment about this," says the disconcerted cop, just shaking his head and waving Ian on.[17]

Throughout this time, Abbot was working on his poetry and writing and poems began to appear in print from 1980 onwards, in *Lines Review, Cencrastus* and *Chapman*. He won two prizes for his poetry, 1st prize of £50 for 'Ariel' in the 1982 'Royal Lyceum Theatre Club Poetry Competition' and 2nd prize of £35 for 'Scott's first voyage' in the 1985 Scottish Association for the Speaking of Verse 'Diamond Jubilee Poetry Competition'. He toured with the Scottish Poetry Library around Scotland in the mid-1980s, giving readings and workshops and in 1987 won a much needed and deserved Scottish Arts Council Bursary which enabled him to focus on bringing the manuscript of *Avoiding the Gods* together, being published by Chapman Publishing in 1988. For his 1985 Scottish Arts Council bursary, Edwin Morgan, another supporter of Abbot's work, provided a reference:

> I have followed Ian Abbot's work with interest as it has appeared in magazines over the last five years or so, and I have also, as a judge, picked out his poetry in competitions. Although he has not so far brought out a book, he now has enough for a collection, and has steadily worked at his

poetry to improve it. His prize-winning poem in the S.A.S.V. competition earlier this year was agreed by Norman MacCaig and myself to be an original and imaginative piece of writing. He is a man who deserves encouragement [...][18]

This application proved to be unsuccessful, but the referee for his 1987 successful application was Tessa Ransford who wrote that 'although so far largely neglected, he [Abbot] is in fact one of our leading contemporary poets' and praised the 'adventurous and contemplative' nature of his poetry.[19] Writing after his death and to his widow, Frances, Ransford hails Abbot as one of her 'favourite' contemporary poets.[20] The circumstances of his death in 1989 have already been covered at the beginning of this introduction but it is worth mentioning that at the time he had been a contender for a Saltire Prize on the strength of *Avoiding the Gods* which 'exhibits a sometimes sombre but graceful muscularity'.[21] Joy Hendry, of *Chapman,* organised a reading to celebrate Abbot's life and work, which was held in Perth on 18 May 1990 and attended by poets such as Raymond Vettesse, Duncan Glen, Alexander Hutchison, George Gunn and Raymond Ross. Edwin Morgan, who could not attend that evening sent an apology and a note to be read out in his absence:

> I am sorry that circumstances have prevented me from attending on this occasion, as I would have wished to pay my respects to Ian Abbot. I remember how, five years ago, I picked out his prizewinning poem when I was judging a competition for the Scottish Association for the Speaking of Verse. It had an original and imaginative touch which made it stand out and stick in the mind. Later I admired how he had developed his sombre, glowing imagination in the collection he brought out in 1988 [...] Ian's untimely death is a loss to Scottish poetry but he has left us a volume which we shall continue to read.[22]

In some of the unpublished poems that follow, Abbot has not provided titles. The notion of the 'untitled' poem is something that resonates in his work, not only his search to learn a new language in the feral landscape but that he was self-made as a poet with very little financial support, or indeed much success until his very last years. Edwin Morgan above pays tribute to Abbot's determination to work at his poetry to improve it, and to do anything that would allow him the time and space to do that. Partly because of where he lived, at a remove from both Glasgow and Edinburgh (a distance he said he regretted in his SAC application) Ian Abbot's was an outsider voice in Scottish poetry. Following his sudden death, his achievement appeared to be frozen in time. The publication of his work here should show how his poetry is one of difference, of standing out, even if that risks neglect, of following a calling no matter what obstacles might stand in the way. This collection also shows its significance and capacity to endure. Colin Nicholson wrote that 'it is hard to think that Ian has gone, and in a sense he hasn't.' Nicholson attributed his ongoing presence to a liberation from life's leading devotions and directions.[23]

Additionally, and finally, Colin Nicholson, in a letter to Abbot dated 12/12/1985, suggests three titles for Abbot's collection of poems: 'Caliban rising', 'Finishing the picture' and 'Avoiding the gods'.[24] While Abbot opted for the latter, a title such as 'Finishing the picture' might have sounded odd for a poet making his first step into book publication. Now, however, given that Abbot's poetry ended so suddenly and tragically in 1989, it seems poignantly fitting to collect Abbot's poems together into one volume, including many poems that have never been published and have been stored at the National Library of Scotland for nearly a decade. That Abbot would have published a follow-up collection to *Avoiding the Gods* is beyond question and in helping to 'finish the picture' of his life and work, it seems reasonable to suggest that he might have become one of Scotland's most celebrated poets.

Richie McCaffery

Note on the text

The full text of *Avoiding the Gods* is reproduced here, with only a handful of typographical errors corrected from the original published version. Every effort has been taken to faithfully reproduce Abbot's poems and titles, but where titles have not been available, the first line of the poem has been inserted, printed in grey. Longer poems that extend over more than one page, necessitating the page to be turned, have been slightly reordered to ensure ease of reading.

Avoiding the Gods 25

Ferns like poems

They rise
out of the earth like innocent serpents set to strike.
Their folded, poisoned heads assume
an attitude of piety; humility of old
is written in the language of their curves.

And you will curse them as they cross your lawns
and run them down, attempt
their sure destruction with machineries
and poisons, with the blind sweep of the scythe.
But they will seed the earth invisibly
and burgeon up again like little nuns
coiled over ancient prayers. I warn you

to approach them with respect.
Carelessly fingered, every cowering stem
will strip you to the bone;
lay your soft hands open.
And innocently celebrate the spilling of your blood.

Forms

Why do these people look at me today?
Why do they look at me and say
that today something has gone out of him, that now
his self is no longer the self that we remember?

Answering this is not easy. I can only say
that to my mind nothing stays as it was. It is true
that the world seems little changed, that trees
are looted still by these October winds, and that the air
beats to the ancient measure of the dance,

and yet the birds
which passed last summer underneath my eaves
did not return this year.
Only their nests remain: abandoned husks
of mud and stick,
held together
by spittle and a few feathers from the breast.

The bestiary of Cortes

Mythical
we move like centaurs
through the fabulous wood.

They come to us
jewelled like birds:
their eyes are downcast, they look into the earth:
mould stirs under their feet.
They come to us
with shields made of feathers,
with armour
made of feathers,
with bones, with souls
made of feathers.

They look on our ships and are amazed: from every tree
their eyes stare down like pearls. I am their god.
None can believe
that everything I am is mortal. They deploy
about my feet their offerings of gold.

And now my pikes split bone from bone
like heavy bills; the sun gorges
on blood and broken plumes, steam
rises from the earth.
A wind stirs my cloak like wings,
my horse is trembling against my thighs.

I move like a centaur through the sullen green.
They see me now.
I am the one, the feathered one,
the black. My heavy bill clacks shut.
I am the raven of Christ.

Montezuma

Blade
of obsidian, handle
of soft green gold. When I bear
the knife aloft I gaze
into the eyes of my own obscure gods.
The altar, the pyramid
are a slow glacier of blood; breaking
the vault of the chest the heart
squirms like a rabbit. I hear
the sun drink its fill
that the earth be renewed. To this end
I move like a lever of the universe, my brain
crawls with calculations.

And to this end I wait for the hour of my own death.
For not till my body rolls from the steps
and slides without effort
into the endless dance of the dead,
till beasts
mouth my famished remains, till the hair of the priests
stinks with my matted blood
will the enigmatic smile
occur about the mouths of the gods
and the earth flourish and bloom.

Maize and water, smoke
of incense of copal await my people at my death.
Till then I bide my time, my arm
falls and rises in the service of the sun.

Vestal

Your flesh is pale, and lit
as if from far within by pure and solemn candles.
Even now, your bloodstream moves
to the meticulous incantations of the mass.
Your breath is the breath of censers, and your glance
the blue of blue smoke coiling upward slowly.

Tell me if we meet here
when we are folded one upon another
silently, and intimate as votive palms;
or if you shelter in some other sacristy? I know
the only body that you know
is that one hacked with nails, and pierced,
and laid out like a specimen across a wooden frame.
And this sequesters me and endless others
even when we stretch above the blind cross of yourself.

He watches from the shadows of the room, and wears
the face you have ascribed to him. Bloodied
with joy, and torn
out of the animal life by ecstasy, he has attained
that consummate and endless martyrdom
your reverential soul is reaching for.

Except that in the end, for you
there is never more
than ancient repetitions in the dark, and at the last
the money spinning on the table, and
the body's bitter vinegar to drink.

Crossing the ford

Late autumn, and the days
go shuffling by on tiptoe
like lines of old, exhausted men.
The sun has spent itself for winter: now it blows
along the low dark line of the horizon,
its late fires
flapping in the trees above the river.
Flecked with white, the water rolls away
the ochres and the crimson, the blood-banners of leaves.

I could say to myself,
"This is perhaps
the way the wicked years have plundered me. Season upon season
the best of me gone
into a falling water, swept away
like little red tongues in a rolling spate."
And nothing left to show for all
the rigid strivings of a life
committed to a catching-up of images, a wintry
flooding out of words.

But I know there are other seasons. Seasons
when a strong fuse splutters in the blood, ignites
the mind to burn its succulent green phrases
into a rising cloud of poems, and reveal
the word-rings thrusting outward under pliant bark.

I feel that verdant smoke blow through me
now in this threadbare time. As a shrinking sun
withdraws its heat, so I watch the river sluice
the glorious dead skin of the year. But now I celebrate
the coming burgeoning of shoots, the words
that wait to blossom at my fingers' ends.

Inside the altarpiece

The terrible angels drop
out of a sky like lead. Their dresses shine
with the many-tinted lustres
of forgiveness, white little harbours
for the sure and penitential man
reveal themselves within
the leaded panels of their wings.
Their voices, singing,
shape their mouths in perfect rounds.

But what have they to say
to those who bruise themselves
against the hard invaginations of their gowns?
What smallest word of solace, peace,
for those who cannot bear
the purity of all this virginal serenity?

None. None. None.
Not a single, simple sound
from them imparts
any show of beauty to the sky
from which they fall, from which their wings
have taken every colour, every tone
which might console us in an hour of desperation.

They pose before the painter, study
their every gesture, and simper
in a way which only favourites can understand.

I say
that their sky is lead, that each
immaculately-painted nail
is no more than a claw
directed at my eyes, and that
the beautiful circles of their mouths
will suck my heart in time:
that my own blood will at last perfect
the simple, terrible beauty of their congregation.

Spoor

There are tracks here in the snow
and in the earth, in the black mud
that the rains have left. A scent, elusive,
lingers in the air, torments
my sense with its familiarity.

I have followed these
for a long time. Whoever
passed this way has not a secret left from me.
Under the sun, under the scintillating wheel of stars
this spoor has learned to talk to me
as clearly as my mother's voice.
Here, he seems
to float almost above the earth: here he has crossed
spates and torrents in a single
spasm of his heart,
while here his toes dig down, his even stride
lengthens like a dog's, and I know
what shadows rise behind him from the dark.
Even now I catch
the sudden, sharp stench of his fear.

His blood
on this black rock, there on a twig
a hair, a fragment of his skin; and I
have built him in my mind from these invisibles.
His walk is like my own: his limbs,
his eyes. He wears my old discarded clothes.

And one day I will catch him on the skyline,
relaxed and unaware, until I raise
the long rifle of language to my shoulder
and hold my breath, and squeeze
and squeeze.

And watch the words like bullets home in for the kill,
and hear
the echoes roll away around the world.

Ariel

A sudden breath, a dark sharp
whispered word, and I
go out into the world like dreams.

The earth below me
passes by like smoke, and as I turn
my head this way and that
there are those who sleep
and those
whom I bring out of sleep; those who are born
into the world and those from whom I draw the world away.

All night, all night
I work in whispers, dreams and air
until the morning brings me back here to your feet.

To feel your collar fixed about my neck
and my soul fastened to the iron in the earth.

Marriages

Under the carapace of snow and ice
a warmth is flaring still in the dark earth.
We have seen it, you and I,
pushing its small and tender
flickering pale celadon
through the mailed fist that grips us: we shout
aloud at all
that tiny life we thought was irretrievable, celebrate
over and over, year after year,
those small forgotten pulsings under the dead snow.

Scott's first voyage

I crouch among the snowfields of my mother's body.
Under the white drifts of her breasts I suck new air
which holds the callousness of blizzards;
which makes my raw lungs freeze and fills my veins
with scintillating quatrefoils of ice. Her distant voice
comes booming in my ears like wind

while here and there the nurses' wicked frosts
go crackling by. Profundity of ice-falls
underlies their intimate sounds; their speech
mysterious, dangerous and flawed as glaciers.
Timidly my nerves reach out and hold.
I guy myself to daylight.

A thin sun slides into the room
along its skate-edge: glittering motes
cascade like atoms through its pane. Mechanically
it moves toward me, passes over me
its thin, slow blade
and marks me for the future.

Now I begin to cry
inside this difficult weather, crouched
within the whiteout of my own new voice.
My body
is a red tent
already stained
with the signatures of a hard passage. It shivers
in the terrible wind of the world and longs
to fly away and lose itself
among the flying shrouds: to fuse its breath
into the rivet-breath of ice.

I ask you sleety angels, starched
in your immaculate pompadours, your
ice-mantillas,
simply to let me be.
I slithered from a cold mother
whose poor, blanched mouth, open
at my birth, delivered frozen vowels,
inarticulate and full
of bleak, frostbitten anger.

That voice drifts still
into the small bones of my ears
as beneath me I feel
my own slow glacier begin to stir
and carry me away,
Embedded like a rock I go
to score myself
along the deep trench of the world, to scratch
a history into
my little history into the bitter landscape waiting.

I ask you sleety angels, starched
in your immaculate pompadours, your
frost-mantillas,
simply to let me be.
I slithered from a cold mother
whose poor, blanched mouth, open
at my birth, delivered frozen vowels,
inarticulate and full
of bleak frostbitten anger.

And that dumb voice drifts still
into the small bones of my ears
as under me I feel
my own glacier begin to stir
and carry me away.
Embedded like a rock I go
to score myself
along the deep trench of the world; at last to scratch
my little history into the bitter landscape waiting.

The last entry of a polar explorer

Surrounded, here,
by these white peaks
the heart itself will turn to ice,
crusted and festooned in anonymous snow.
To me it is like
the sight of your body shrinking into distance,
your white hand waving from its furs.

You talked to me
of roots and fires, of tiny feathers
and of tiny deaths, of all the minute life
that rages under these terrible white horizons.
I can only say
that each of these small losses fades
beside the manner
in which every intricate memory of you
will be lost with my loss,
a perfect likeness
taken down under the snow with me, a burial-prize.

Through my head
a language runs which I have never spoken.
Full of high, strange syllables and broken vowels,
deciphered from the blizzard and the heaving ice,
it is a final language that I understand.
Often now it whispers to me quietly:
talks of my own white body dwindling
and of how far down these endless drifts will bury you.

A crofter buried

To wade at last
in the soft ocean of the earth, finally to see
how your every tentative step
has been preserved, infolded:
and to notice
how they form one singular, uncertain track
that leads back all the way to your beginnings.

Your children carry you above ground. Through stones
and over dark, low bushes.
Now you move
in wood and brass while under and between
your body and their solemn legs
the warm air trembles like a sheaf.

You thought to print the earth indelibly.
But now let down, and burdened
with the bare field's sullen weight,
you must lie still and be content.
The cairn begins to crumble
even as the final stone is being placed.

Your footprints are already blowing shut.
In time the earth accepts from you
the price of everything you borrowed from it.

A body of work

Do you not see, finally,
how the earth is moving to inhabit me?

My teeth
are the white stones of the river-bed;
throughout the day
an otter dozes in the dank holt of my mouth.
The sinews of my legs
go down into the earth like roots, and knots of shifting clay
compose the muscles of my face.
My hair, my sex becoming
clumps of hoary winter grass.

Seasons are manifest in me:
I know their white, their green, their turning yellow.
Laughing, my voice is the fever of stags; the pure
transparency of leaves is in my speech. Constellations
sift their burning atoms through my veins.

But in singing, weeping,
waking in the night and crying out,
my language is a deer dismembered under pines,
bloody and netted with shadows.
An intricate labyrinth of entrails,
lit from within
and patiently transfigured to the lightning grin of bones.

Caliban rising

Bright Ariel, the fresh springs of my heart
are rising in their own white torrent after heavy rain.
A sky which seemed
endlessly to be cast in dull and lightless metal
now at last is cracking open. Water in the air
will flood my throat
with half-forgotten, half-remembered words.

How long I planned against that old magician of the mind!
So delicately, and without
the slightest attitude of haste
I countermined his river-courses,
wormed his banks with labyrinths,
unpicked each clotted drain and rearranged
the settled silt of years

till now above the red banks, over the banks
which are gripped and knitted
in a filigree of roots, and bound
and shuttered in the deep
solemnity of sodden earth, your own bright voice
is singing to me like the voice
of runnels burgeoning with tiny, tumbling vowels
and froth of consonants. A breath of water
set you free, and frees my suddenly
from sweating, vegetable banks I moved between. Now I will raise
a new vocabulary out of this white spate. Now I will speak
of air and the tumult of cataracts.
Now I will cover the earth.

And sooner or later, when the waters fall
I'll find his old cloak drying on a tree, washed clean
of all its old mysterious signals; torn
to nothing more than crow-rags,
rotted and flayed by stones.

Then you will live in me at last, my Ariel,
and I will take you, body and spirit,
to roam my real inheritance: my language
glittering like coins beneath the watered sun.

Ewe against the fence

A blue daubed-sheep is haunting the garden,
determinedly tearing a late meal
out of the wasted grass.

It stares at me from somewhere
far behind its stricken, armoured face
with the worn look of an actor
who has endlessly rehearsed
a lifelong role of innocent surprise.

Animal, you do not fool me
for an instant. I see
how your jaws move like machinery,
how your lowered, humble head
in time will scour the green ground into dust,
and how you try
to camouflage your origins with a smear of woad.

I would remind you that you are
a stranger here.
And if I must recall
the vanished voices from my history, and assume
some portion of the dead weight of their passing,
then I call on you
to think of those who have been launched into the dark
before the careless patter of your feet, the endless
rolling phalanx of your horns.

That ever-breaking wave of bone has carried them away
into obscurity. I warn you now
to ponder where you place
you hard, fastidious limbs,
your ceaseless mouth.
The voices of the dead will rise about you

like those mute, white moths disturbed in heather.
Listen to them. Do not think you are alone
in giving up your bones, your flesh,

your blood or destiny to those
who might supplant you with the turning of a coin.

Avoiding the gods

They have come
to scald our blood, to call us out
from our bright houses to the twisted shadows under trees.
Let us not listen to them. Do not let them in.

There beyond the darkened garden, in the obscure forest,
the night expends itself in numberless small deaths.
That is the way of them, the way of predators. A kind
of innocent destruction
but destruction nonetheless.

Let us abandon them
to moulder on their crosses,
beat their iron wings; to redeploy their armies and invent
new forms of sinning and guilt.

Let us remain here, calmly
taking bread, and wine, and speech.
And in the morning
take our limbs to work, and walk behind
the swaying, fuming breath of cattle.

And let us look for our salvation
in the language we have come to teach ourselves.

Before the flood

River of ice,
the brittle lights of winter burn in you
even in the swarming heat of summer.

Behind the livid flush of heather, under
the motionless roots of hills, you drag
your tiny, chiding voice
that speaks to us
only of the bleak privations of the past, that nettle
flowering still out of the dark silt of your throat.

Deer lap your surface, out of your summer depths
the muscled trout come rising after blue, staccato flies
while hopeful boys throw webs across your skin.
Birds hang above you; day by day
the kestrel and the shrew perform
their intricate, ancient measure by your edge.

You watch them with your glacial eye.
Your patient sinews gather, and your bed
can feel the first autumnal heavings.
Soon that chorus of the voices from the past will rise
and roll down in your belly, while carcasses

of sheep and men
will swim in all your exultation,
yawing on your face like dirty clouds.

The suicides of April

This catastrophic spring is loosed on us at last.
After the cool syllabic winter, when every voice
fell like crystal down
through air composed of brilliants; held
in the lucid certainties of frost and ice
a single limpid tone, now a tumult
of rushing voices rushes over us.

In all this quarrelsome language we can feel
how the blood burns now as it once slept
through still December's single note, and how
the mind broadcasts its curious desires. We do not sleep
as we did then, unencumbered through the frost; now the air
displays for us the sickest visions of the heart.
Night and day are one, and both dissolve
in the riotous discords of the mouth.

The turbulence of growth is hard. The music
of the season surges through the earth; a desperate
raging after life informs its difficult harmonies.
But harder still is that
devotion to the stasis of the single voice, the aria perceived
behind the clamour of the cymbals and the horns.

The voice of winter lingers on in us: we hold and hold
to that one fading melody. Little by little
it sinks beneath the brute orchestral chaos, till at length
it dwindles into silence, overwhelmed as we are now
by the rising murderous rapture of the spring.

An inland sea

Morning
The glass, this morning, is a vision of the sea.
A pale light flickers on its surface, makes of its plane
a pool of fluid motion, where my own face
swims in uncertain water like a shoaling-buoy.

Light crusts the water-surface, light informs
the moods I find reflected in its depths. Where today
my image founders in a sea of brass,
so tomorrow
it may be virginal, serene; even at noon
a phosphorescent evening sea might bear me up.

Afternoon
This mirror-light makes prisms of my flesh.
Bones, blood and heart transfigured now
into a whimsical scaffolding of rays;
a lit, triumphal column of the mirror-sea.
my face dissolves
in solemn carnivals of lights, reflections;
in the glassy darkening of calms.

Evening
The ghost behind the mirror
flickers at the edge of sight. The shark, forgotten,
muscles its hungers from the deepest floors
and spirals up in silence: the very soul of the abyss
comes rising at the dusk, the innocence
of long ago.
It courses there below the perfect skin, the balm
and reassurance of this inland sea. The evening's glitter
blinds me.
Only now, and now, in glimpses
of that familiar sail do I recall
what lies beneath the swell, the mouth
that waits there to devour the world.

I – The astrologer

Master, I see you tranced
before the orbits of the planets
as, cloistered in your scholar's gown,
you stumble to divine
the prophecies of ancient stars.

Your room is cheerless, clad
in stony, celibate grey. The floor
is quarried from the earth, red dirt,
where dogs go thrashing after splintered bones.
While you sit

on a throne of shaven wood,
and musing on the orb that swings above your head.
The future, spun
into a globe of gold, with constellations stitched
in diamonds, rubies, emeralds across its face.
Master, you seek
to navigate the firmament,
to map the future like a sounding-chart.

But now observe this globe I offer you.
A globe of dirtied bone, that bears
across its dome
a web of intricate sutures that will speak to you
as all the choiring voices of the planets never could.

I hold for you
the one truth of the future, spun
in two blank orbits you will come to sail at last.
I warn you that the sure tide of the universe
is beating, cased in ivory, between my hands.

II – The knight

He came
with burnished armour buckled tight about him,
shivering the light, and mounted
on that great war-stallion like a battlement, whose long tread
set a movement trembling in the earth. His gilded pennant
flung its silk against the wind, the motion
of his long sword flickered through the bright air like a flame.
He sang a battle hymn of generations.

I named him, and delivered
all the ancient rituals of combat. Then I poured
the ruin of my black breath on him in a wave

and watched his damascene corrupting into dust. Years
fell on him in moments, and his terrible strength
went bleeding out from him into dust
that parted to receive his broken frame.
I picked my way among the splinters of his lance
and tied his pennant, smeared
with stains of many victories, around my waist.

Then rode his spavined horse away, forgetting him,
and quietly humming snatches of his glorious, martial song.

III – The Queen

Sexless, I move
among her languid women.
Cowled in blue, the colour
of the virgin, so I lead her
where her lowered train disturbs
a scent of camomile above the lawns,
above the margin of the long pit waiting.

Her shuttered summers burn beneath the cloisters
and the air
is stunned with heat
while far above her head
the great wild sickles of the swifts go reaping.

Now at the edge she smiles, and turns her gaze
toward the locked gate fastened in the wall.
Her virgins creep like stones. I take her hand.
I tell her, "Here there is another way.
Come with me now. Come down with me. Come down."

Shrapnel

It came to him, he said,
one white night in an empty,
frozen desert of his youth
as he stood lost beneath a sky
that fumed with clouds of seeding stars.

Some cometary debris,
flung outwards from
the great, elliptical orbiting of wars
brushed by him, pressed
its glittering needles through his flesh

and pinned him down.
But he remembered nothing of it
till he woke uneasily
among the charred bones
and the ruinous, subsiding light of fires.

Then later, someone drew
those tiny spittings out of him, except
for one deep splinter, just
too intimately-placed
to tease away with safety.

So now he bears it with him, inoffensive
for the most part, quiescent
other than on nights like this
when we sit by and watch again
his blank eyes flicker

as that old recording whirls in him,
spinning its terrible roll
of names, and sounds, and silenced voices.
His unforgetting needle twists and shifts itself; minutely
scratching, scratching at his heart.

One place in the Highlands

This is a land familiar with destruction.
The low hills, brows beaten down,
and the stubborn, ravaged crags
speak of it, each in its own inimitable voice.
A tired murmur
floats across harsh, unshakeable silences.

Among them
men go trailing after sheep, in company
with dogs that drag their bellies on the earth.
Their speech
has sunk beneath the stridency of flocks
and even now, unguessed, their blood retains
some essence of the old calamities: a sediment
of smoke and broken roof-trees and the covering snow.

The voices of the land invade their sleep.
Night after night
the still, insistent whispers
tell of the life gone out of it,
of every irrecoverable absence.
When these men dream, they dream themselves
the residue of calumny.
The final, tumbled stones of ancient derelictions
and remembered deaths.

Landscape of a Highland gentleman [26]

A dried-up river bed,
the mind of this old man
spreads the bone-white of its boulders in the sun.

He has forgotten, now, how once
these gulleys wrestled with the fever of the spate,
how suddenly in spring
the banks blazed into green, and how
the drinking deer
printed the sand with their perfect arrowheads.

Now he sighs, turns over, shuts his eyes
on that ravine of polished stones. He listens
for the wind's dry rattle, for the quiet
sift of pebbles.
He will close his ears
to the corrie's fistful of silence.

Tick

At first it's all head and no body,
you're burdened with profitless limbs and voracious jaws.
Then comes a time
when you bury your head in the world and begin to feed:
slowly at first, then more and more explicitly
till finally your body lifts behind you like an airship,
swollen by the nothingness of experience, your head a microdot.

That's the time to let go, and to begin
the seemingly endless tumble to the ground.
You crawl off somewhere quiet, start
to digest what you've ingested. Then suddenly,
all at once, the poem comes.

And you're back to square one: body
shrunken to a pinhead, enormous mouthparts
churning at the air. You lie low for a while, getting hungrier,
then creep
to some concealed but advantageous spot.
Here all you can do is wait. Wait
until some fleshy, unsuspecting corner of the world draws near.

The beetle man

Little victor,
black and shining,
whose incendiarist's eyes reduce to silence
even the most callous of his nurses,
kneels now in the corner. Head bent,
arms raised aloft, he hoists
the unendurable weight of the earth between his shoulders.

He carries this all day. But later,
waking in the dusk, he comes to realise
that what he bears upon his back
is no more than the smallest ball of dung –

fragile and sodden with tears
but radiant,
the Little Victor's own true face,
and phosphorescing in the failing light.

Promenaders on the tideline

Under the immense winter sky
the couples go hand in hand along the beach.
Now across the sea, now over the land
their gazes sweep like searchlights:
they do not see each other, do not speak, alike
through rubbish and through razor-glass
their feet wander in unison.

The colour of the sea is red, the land is black.
Both are featureless, and between
these two apparent symmetries the couples shuffle to and fro.
Isolated, each heart
beats to its own sea-rhythm, every head
will net its shoals of dreams and small desires, and only where
the fingers mesh does one world
break upon another,
the couples moving on the tideline
through the woven litter of the land and sea.

Each symmetry
is minute, inviolate; becoming one
only where these exhausted forms are intertwined.

Digging for victory

It was the early, sleep-filled songs of finches
or the sudden bite
of ivory sunlight on the wall that broke on me
and hauled me, drugged
and half-awake into the day
after a long night's luckless rooting among words.

A mile away, beneath
its travelling cloud of gulls,
a miniature blue tractor led a plough
through the steps of combing green earth into brown
by thin degrees. Plumes of smoke
and engine-roar set a harsh music rising in the air.

And at that moment I believed
I saw the way the dance of poetry should go.
The mind's share delving in the tumbled ground
of language, and the smooth poems
furling out behind it, in a wake
of ever-breaking waves –

their rich, oiled sillions
curved away across the earth, and all caught up
in great, symphonic workings of the heart.
But this grim dream passed over me in moments. Turning
from the window I prepared
the clumsy, long-familiar tools

and set again to hacking at reluctant roots.

Hephaestus preaching [27]

His brow a rod of iron. When he speaks
his jaw and cheekbones ring with the sonority of bronze.
A hard gleam from the window burnishes his hair
and his blue vision smokes like sapphires, torn
out of the earth by sweat of muscle and mind.

His god is not the god who comes
in poor humility,
spiralling downward, dovelike,
to croon us tales of goodness and the power of love:

his demon falls in brass and damascene,
ravages the transgressor with his light
and comes down in a long, barbaric clamour
while this servant pours the molten metal from his mouth.

Yet, when the judgement is delivered here, and fists
like gavels cease to pound the pulpit-rim,
he will succumb to a familiar alchemy
and wander from the church on limbs of lead

palsied and trembling, helped
by pink-faced boys who chatter
to an old, exhausted man

and lead him home, then run out
innocent as gold,
and roar their own seditious sermons in the street.

Ward Seven — December

Sudden laughter
rattles
in the ward
        and
                fine bones of spring rain
                swing
                in the winter wind
        but
round this bed
there is only
silence
and the numbed quiet
of snow.

Ian R. H. Abbot

Ward seven – December

Sudden laughter
rattles
in the ward

and
fine bones of spring rain
swing
in the winter wind.

but
round this bed
there is only
silence
and the numbed quiet
of snow.

Exile

They have murdered me here on this raw plain:
dismembered, my body lies beneath the earth.
The brittle heat of summer, the winter's acid rain,
all are alike to me in this disguise. Above my head
curlew and plover
draw their sad lines from one horizon to another.

To fill my mouth with stones and to invest
my body with the degradation of the soil they feel
will quiet me at last. They listen
to every nuance of the wind, to each
minute design of cloud and leaf they give a rapt, particulate concern.
In the absolute silence
of these scrubbed hills they are content
that they have laid me finally to rest.

But wait. Only wait.
For as each drop of water comes
through years of effort trickling down
to my dry lips, so words
go welling upwards through the earth,
brimming at last into a lake of poems.

They will have forgotten where they buried me.
But one day, passing, they will see
how waterfowl go shrieking at the sky and how
the boulders tremble in their beds and cry aloud.

A cancelled poetry lesson

Dear Mrs. ---, I ask you not to send
your daughter to attend today. My own prognosis
for the afternoon is bad.

There are some days
when great clouds build up in the mind. Gorged with dark
and faintly lit about their rims with lurid pastels, they presage
the advent of a dreadful, pressing weight of snow.

And under them my words and phrases slink away
into impenetrable thickets, go down deep
and huddle there in silence.
On other days I might have sent
my wicked, private terriers tunnelling
to flush them out, and rip them to the surface

but now they also languish in their kennels,
ill at ease and shaking with uncertainty.

So do not send
your little girl today. Tomorrow may be better,
but my prognosis for this afternoon is bad.

Drawing to a close

I am an old man now. My eyes are weak
and all my vision blurred like an ancient photograph.

Only when I close my eyes, only when I sleep
can I recall things as they used to be.
The pure curves of the palette, soft
and rounded as the body of the virgin
I watched them pull once from the river.
Her limbs held such repose, such tones
of pearl-white, alabaster, ivory,
that ever afterwards I moved towards my palette like her lover
and would not paint
until I felt its fine wood tremble in my hands,
its bleached-white body breathing into mine.

I laid my colour out along its edge
like eyes, or like small milestones to the stations of my soul.
The bitter joy of yellows, moving in me
like the sudden turning of her arms above the chains;
the wicked ochres spreading through my blood
in just the same way
that the shadows of her dead hair
bled into the sullen water. And I tell you
that I painted exultation
from the wide, religious blue of her gaze, coloured
like the lapis that I laid down then across the palette's rim.

But now, awake and old, her image fades from me
like antique sepia. While my palette,
battered driftwood, bears
dead shards if colour I can only blend to river-silt.

I watch my vibrant brushes drowning in a jar.
I do not think that I will take them up again.

Blizzard conditions [28]

Snow lowers its curtain.
Winter falls like an axe.

The wreaths of summer, and
the many-headed riot of the spring,
the slow corruption of October,
all lie alike
beneath the simple competence of snow.
Loss is in it;
yours and mine. Loss
and desolation
lurk beneath its bland apologies.

Trees break under its weight.
So, you and I,
spreading our hopeful needles
ultimately falter and fall.
Our roots bear down on ice, and nothing rises
out of the frozen earth that we can hold.

We sit before the fire, and platitudes
slowly begin to cover us. Dreaming
of spring and radiance, all we know
is nothing but the slow, encroaching cold.

This loss of feeling
rises in the earth of you and I
and nothing any more remains
of warmth and tumult: nothing more
of bloom, and consummation, and decay.

One season gathers round us like a fist.
One merciless winter language squeezes us like ice.

43

The oriental archer

The rituals delivered, now he draws
the great yew bow in silence
and settles in a stillness which is absolute.

Minutes grow like moss, and imperceptibly the room
becomes a quiet centre of the world.
Within the arc of bow and string
the constellations gather, poised
along the perfect fulcrum of the shaft
that all his will is centred on.
Slowly the man invades the bow
that fuses with the sinews of his arm; his own blood
thrums on the string's nerve
drawn from his own still body, circling the earth.

At length, unnoticed,
the struggle over and its purpose gone,
the arrow slips away
to its unfathomable destination. It leaves behind
a perfect synthesis
of man and bow and star;
a single interlocking form
that hold the crowd
illumined on the edge of mysteries.

So that even when he leaves the stage
the room is still. The placid air
still murmurs with the endless motion of the bow.

Agates

The language lies in the road like stones
pitted and ordinary;
kicked by every passer-by
and crammed in dykes, and tumbled
upside-down in a thousand meaningless cairns.

Only pick it up and split it, polish it
over and again
with dust and finer dust and patience,
and hold it up at length against the light.

Then you will find its unseen, echoing rings.
Then you will see how its limitless rainbows
irradiate the world, your substance, and your ordinary skin.

Quiet evenings at home

In the solemn hour when the moon rises;
the late moon, the sonorous copper moon of autumn
that floods the heart directly
with its secretive, magnetic tides,
then the streets fill slowly with abandoned light.

A screech owl utters the first speech of the dead
and you and I,
alone and fused beneath the blankets
feel the touch of history, the future,
go passing over us like wings
beating the flooded air, moving their shadows
into the secret, smallest corners of the room.

The sailor's widow embroidering

The beach is spread
like a blanket laid down in the sun to dry.
At noon, the whiteness of its cloth is inexpressible

but as the tide advances,
stitch by stitch
encroaching on the fabric of the sand,
so the pure line of its brightness fades
to a glimmering stain, sunk in dusk
beneath the fretted shallows.

She works slowly, frowning, covers
minutely the shrinking borders of her life's blanket
with a tight fretwork of laces: bright
infrequent workings of thread-of-gold, the great
sombre passages of half-remembered remnants.
Invisibly
she pares the last virginal margin
of a cloth inexpressibly white.

Soon she will reach the hem, the beach
vanished at last
under the surface of a sea confused with clouds.

Death watch

In hollow corners of the night
you hear his tiny time-bomb run its course.
Behind the flare of sooty candles, far beyond
the still feet of the dead
his patent-leather metronome is counting down.

Life shrouds the corpse
like plaster smoothed on by an undertaker:
sillion of exhausted hair
is intricately furrowed on the skull; the sunday suit
is blemishless, its careful folds
come near to speaking of vitality: white hollowly over the heart
a pocket-handkerchief lifts three white peaks.

He stares through these illusions, shovels them aside
like moist brown debris from his workings. His mandibles
machine them in and he excretes them in a wake
which smells of breath of incense, gleams
like passages of weeping eyes.
Powered by lust, his body's clock
goes ticking through its doll's-house labyrinth.

The candles gutter in a draught; their flames'
uncertain yellow spreads a black
conundrum fading in the air.
Already your image is settling on the corpse.
Already your bones
are the bones of your children, seated by trestles
and smoothing your stray hairs, polishing your profile
to its final smile.

And listening
to that tiny timepiece in its panelled box
come tapping through their universe. Listening
to their own coiled lifesprings'
slow unspiralling
and their whispering candles gently burning down.

Lament of the horse-bit

I heard its voice
almost before I found it, lying
half-concealed beneath a tumbled cairn of stones.

Its speech
was of the long, complaining moan of harnesses,
the quiet thunder
and the thud and stumble of the plough. A keening
like the cries of spring gulls
circled in its rings,

still linked together
with placental iron, split
and twisted in the forge
to slide between the yellow teeth,
the soft, erotic lips.

It told me of the great, plumed fretlocks
thrashing at the earth, it whispered
of the battering of hearts.

And then I towed it jangling
behind the tractor, letting the long field
burnish it to ancient silver:
an antique, pitted gleam
that now is speaking to me
in an altered voice.

Talking to me of the death of labour
and the emptying of purpose, the demise
of open joy. And crying now,
and railing out against
the sleepless marching of the world.

Laurel bush

One day we will look into the laurel bush.
One day we will peer into its depths
and see the savage green eyes
of the tiger that is lying at the bottom.

We will watch the tremblings
of his long striped body
and taste the odour of his breath.
We will become aware that the shimmering of the bush
which we discerned from far away
is merely the reflection
of sunlight on his prismatic claws.
We will hear the blood
flow through his veins and the veins of leaves.
In his gut and under the bark of the bush
the tunnelling of larvae will become apparent.

Then we will go home to bed, our skins
touching and clinging while the moon
throws shadows of laurel leaves across the walls.
Dreaming the same dream, of the laurel bush
flowering upwards, higher and higher
till the body of the tiger,
stretching in a curve from horizon to horizon,
settles down at last among the stars.

A search for lodgings

You come to my door crying in the night.
Beyond the spilled light lying on the grass,
barely invisible you send your voice to me.

I cannot let you in. Although
your voice is the voice of women I have loved,
although it is the voice of my father and my mother,
although it talks to me
of the smallest, foetal secrets of my heart
in a pleading voice I know to be my own,
the chain must stay on the door and the door stay shut.

I cannot let you in. Cannot
let you in.
For when the grave stares at me beyond the ring of light,
when the night is full of whispers,
when the smell of death
pours like a wind out of your black space,
how can I let you in?

Fishing through a hole

All day I crouch upon
this frozen landscape of the mind. Work hard
but clumsily to bait the tacky iron of the hooks.
The hole I hacked stares back at me, and endlessly translates
the deep obsidian glitter of its lights.

Here on the floes the world is pure.
The brittle air unfolds itself
prism on prism
to the very edge of the horizon.
I am the only thing that moves: all day I drop
my loaded hooks down into the sea's black eye.

I know that underneath me go,
sheltered by the shelving ice,
those real and imagined monsters that the water hides.
And these are what I bait for. The smooth seal's
studded jaw; its broad, rapacious motion through its element.
The penguin's pantomime ferocity, and every simple terror
of a single brain of fish
that panics with one movement in the luminous dark.
Blood shuttles through them all. Their real and cavernous hearts
encompass all desire.

Out of the clarity of ice I sink
a weighted line of words,
a bait of succulent rhythms,
while here in the cold wind of the mind I wait
for that familiar, curious tug. The first
uncertain motion that the world makes
when it feels the barb between its teeth
and rises at the awkward space I made.

And all along the taut line
fireworks up in spray, to burst at last across the hole's bright lip.
The poem is landed red and breathing, smeared with rainbows:
and every burning colour
is mirrored endlessly among the vistas of the bergs.

Sloughing

I am casting off my former lives.
They lie there in the corner
shimmering like the intricate
skins of pythons
or the fabulous Chinese suit of jade.
They regard me like the hollow forms of dead men.

As the earth whirls
on its huge magnetic spindles
so I see
than an infinite procession of minute events
has led me to this moment,
this clamorous afternoon,
and to the company of these abandoned selves.

The past
is deliquescing on the floor,
the present floods in at the window.
Only the future remains inscrutable,
locked up
in a universe that branches like a tree of blood.

Fever

The earth moves in its sleep.
A gold haze spreads over the corn, along
the broken wall where the adders lie.
You caress
their dark diagonals, their wicked heads
pressed flat against the sand.
The immense heat presses down.

Caught in this red light
the river drains into its bed.
The sky
is running away, sounds
of late bells drift like smoke

across the corner of the field
where that remorseless dog goes running
evening after evening
in a straight line towards the horizon.
His red tongue hangs from his mouth like meat
and the scent of him is in the air
for a long time after he has gone.

Wax resist [29]

Beneath your eyes, and under
the solemn ridges of your cheekbones
it is possible to trace,
in the proper light and given
certain innocent defects of the vision,
the spectral echoes of the imprints of my thumbs.
Barely visible, they have etched their way
into the very substance of your face. Now they have become
a necessary element in the definition of your singular beauty.

While I examine myself before the mirror. My body
is naked as a fish. Nowhere
on thigh, or face, or belly do I see
the faintest printing of another hand;
not a loop or whorl which might reveal
the mingling of another psyche with my own.

Clean as a candle I take my blind way through the world
while losses gutter behind me,
and my own thick tears precipitate like wax.

Last dip of the year [30]

Her body was as shy as berries when she stepped
as neatly as a hind out of the bush
she had unrobed in.

And stood there trembling on the edge
above the careless water, summoning
her little courage for the cold plunge.

Till at length she jumped, and folded
all her innocence
into the clear hands of the river.

Her tiny, berry-crimson breasts flared out
like signals from the cool depths, warning
of another season's turning and the spates to come.

A vanished poet's house

I found it many years ago
in a dark mid-morning, on a day
of driving, bitter rain.

It bulked down in the dripping peat, crouched
on four squat walls of whinstone
and somehow almost somnolent, enduring
in the way that cattle do
the shrill, insistent hammering of squalls.

Slowly I circled its patient faces, rubbed
for my eye
a hole in the calendar of a window
and watched my vision slither in
like a rat crossing the floor
to where the date-stone lay,
broken in three and quietly
drifted round with dust.
It bore a skull, a bell, a mason's hammer
crudely worked. The grave
initials chiselled in its face were mine.

I listened to its language, took to myself
a rhythm from its trickling lintels and its broken eaves,
built out of the harsh tongues of its stones
a hoard of phrases of my own:
encountered words like ancient weapons hidden in its thatch.

I looted that house many times,
and piece by piece its vanished voice
renewed itself in mine;
but I will make my final visit when
knocking and knocking on the abandoned door
I hear the echo of my hand

go running through from empty room
to empty room. Then sink down
all at once into the crowded shadows
and sit there motionless.
Holding its breath.
Waiting for me to leave.

Lifeline

The ancient reel goes spinning. And the line,
shot forward from the rod, describes
its momentary pencil-mark across the sky,

looping and swinging, tremulous with life,
until the glittering surface breaks and drags it down.

The deepest water is unknowable. All we remember
is that fragile motion and the rainbow
falling from the line, the bright lure's
trembling flight and fall.

And underneath it all
the old reel's hungry clicking, counting off the days.

Monster

Its body has become
a repository of legends.
Dreams and old personae
lodge beneath its scales: they glitter faintly,
drift loose now and then
and spiral to the bottom and the mud.

Its head
shaped, dully, like a thumb. Seen
by the odd, tranced soul a greenish leather
coats its bones. The eyes bulge out,
its odour is corrupt: no-one has seen it who has not
been filled with loathing and a sense of loss.

Beneath the waves it hangs still like a sad balloon,
stares down toward the distant bottom.
Perhaps it weeps, cries out
in its unimaginable voice. The shores
glitter with shoals of eyes. It knows, one day,
this weight of dreams will pull it down to die.

The shadow-wolf

Today is the day of delusions.
Today is the day
when the shadow-wolf below the stairs becomes the wolf.

Periodically,
messengers come to tell us
in spellbound voices
how the shadow
is composed of innocence, a kind of dream
like butterflies or birds, flying
in the firelight from a pair of hands.
But hearing his rapacious voice, listening
to his breath and smelling
his pelt and the odour of blood
we cannot choose but to believe in the wolf.
We must stay alert all day
while he moans insatiably at the door.

We know, we know
that tomorrow all will be well.
We will come down and see,
as we were promised,
the shadows of simple objects on the wall.
Tomorrow is to be the day of reassurance.

But today is a bad day,
the day of delusions.
Today is the day
when the shadow-wolf rises up and howls.

Ga-Cridhe

A spear once passed among the hands of heroes.
It came to each one
hooded and laced in leather, thonged
and tightly bound about its shaft.
A monk-spear, a spear without a voice,
nevertheless it trembled imperceptibly
throughout the body of the man who carried it.

So that at a certain time, inexorably,
his fingers would unravel ancient knots
and slowly slip the hood
until the head emerged, barren
as the colour of the moon
and studded randomly with bright, barbaric rivets.

Then the voice of the spear would issue from its mouth:
a voice of ruin, hoarse
with the colour of blood. Tumultuous with destruction
it would shout in his mind like the sea
and drive him like an animal
while his companions gathered and stood by,
nodding their grey heads sadly.
Until at length, sated with calamity
the man and the spear lay down together,
and waited to be cowled again with piety and guilt.

And now this spear, or one of its descendants, lives with me.
I keep it hooded: day by day investigate
the safety of its thongs.
But late at night, in sleep
I feel that same spear tremble like a foetus. My dreams
are a complex maze of leather, filled
with patterns of interwoven lines. The thongs
whisper to me, and stained
with the mythical colour of blood
my hands rehearse a slow untying of the knots.

Crossing Carn Donnachaidh

Now at last I have arrived between the double bridges,
where the white burn splits and surges
off to two distinct points of the compass. Here is where
each thread of it begins to learn a new name
and to assume
a form laid down by centuries. To cultivate
a love for certain stones and hollows, and to drop down
roaring into splendid chasms in the earth: or to subside
without complaint among the unacknowledged wastes of hags.

I listen to the double bridges thrumming in the wind.
Their thin, slung sinews and their juggled planks
persuade me of the ordinary, feeble nets
I throw across the world from day to day.
And day in, day out, ponder
which is the proper bridge to cross, which glittering thread
I should adopt and follow to its end.

To resonate the passion of that livid water, and to scour
the deep lines of my signature on stones? Or to persist
in delving softly through the damp ground,
nosing my way in silence:
bleeding out at last into a marsh of words
but unattended, solitary,
and rendered nameless even on the maps.

Bird's eye view

I have been told
that all around, the infinite cage
is barred in starry metal. Tasting
of iron, tasting of water and grain
and smelling of the odours of the body

it stretches from me to the farthest horizon:
within it the constellations burn away, the moon
navigates its cataract.

While here on the sandy bottom
night after night
I blunder like a linnet with its eyes put out.
Bruised and disfigured, terrified to move,
but singing and singing through interminable dark.

Brain coral

Atom by atom, grain by grain,
the reef strives upward at the light.
Its roots lie far below, sunk
in the glimmering memory of the ocean floor; it is sustained
only by numberless tiny deaths, nevertheless
a desperate life invests
its intricate, slow progression.

Familiar charts reveal to me
its broadest contours, but within
its infinite complexities my newest map is obsolete.
I explore it anchored on the slenderest of threads, pass
in and out among its labyrinth of doors.

A dark life underlies
the beauty of its ornament. Behind
the veils of angel fish I smell
the blood-trail of the shark, the hunger
that is never satisfied. Claws
move among the fronds, the whole reef
whispers to the bone-rattle of crabs. Deep
in the radiant pit of the anemone
waits the moray's bleak unlockable jaw.

In a shattering of bubbles I traverse
the reef from end to end; and find at last, along its edge,
above the vague, vertiginous abyss,
the first few hungry stars.
The creeping vanguard of that crown of thorns.

A late note from a prodigal

A glimmering dusk is hanging
just outside the window, pierced vaguely
by a murky glint of stars. A hint
of constellations there, but half-obscured
by the intrusive afterglow of sun.
Father, this is the hour
when predators will raise their heads
and start out on the trail of blood.

And this, too, is the hour
when you and I have always come
together, with myself part-blinded
in your lingering radiance, all your pointers
difficult to follow, incomplete.
You know this time, that animal odour.
It rises from me every time we meet.

But now, at last, with your light dwindling,
might we not move together
into an honest, proper dark?
Your constellation laid out
like a flarepath still could let me learn
to navigate myself
towards a landfall you could come to understand.

Rites of passage

Last night the profoundest angel,
the voiceless Azrael, passed this way.
I found his mark this morning on my door,
barely discernible, but doubtless. Almost concealed
in the cabbala of the frost,
but speaking to me in a voice devoid of mystery,
it revealed to me the advent of my own death.

I went at once to the oldest people, being concerned
to report what I had seen. Each regarded me placidly,
without emotion; but listening intently, their ancient eyes
reverberating lamplight. Then suddenly
an old one drew me aside. His hair was white,
his face drained as a ditch, his teeth
had vanished long ago when all the gold of them was stolen.
He suffered.
"You have seen what you believe
to be the signature of angels.
A frost-mark burned across your door; the fingerprint of Azrael?

"I tell you now that I have seen his face. He left no traces.
His eyes were blue as beryls, and he wore
unparalleled drapery of silver and of black, while from his thighs
sprang hounds with mouths of ivory, tireless and inestimable.
He carried lightning on his shoulders, gathered
thousands in the turned cuff of his sleeve. They passed
into oblivion.

"And I survived. These others here
survived. But the stench of his breath is on us
and we smell it on our dreams
and in our dreams we are no longer living. In our dreams
we are charred by frost and we are burned: we have been ploughed
into the mulch of Europe."

I heard him out politely, then returned home.
And opened my door and laid away
the incantations and the talismans with which
I once believed that I could arm myself.
For I know that he is coming. Coming quietly, and without
the clamour of machinery or dogs. Sooner or later,
one day he will enter as a traveller might,
asking for directions or a little food.

Then, resting both his hands in mine
will draw me through my doorway,
smiling at me like a distant friend
and calmly pointing me the way.

A late note to my mother

The tune of the harp is driven
onto the mean trees of this season.
A long tune, green
with grace notes even in the frost, it will sustain
its delicate harmonics through whatever bitter weather
seeks to chill the heart of it.

I tell you
that your life is wrapped in mine: and even as
these live, unseasonable branches
still are splendid under snow, so
the smallest veins of you extend their song
into my song. Your heart in mine, a throne of strings
whose singing voice will still be heard
long after the cooling earth
has taken both of us into its ice.

The mechanisms of the gin

Sixteen teeth, set
in a lurid, iron smile.
Chained to the earth, anchored
into black soil, nonetheless
its everyday, simple grin sustains itself.

Its mouth spills feathers.
White bones tumble from it
one upon another: numberless
but laid like runes across the ground.
The great jaw of the badger, skull of the grouse,
an endless filigree of weasels. Yearly
it raises cairns that honour
no more than its own eternal memory.

You tend it with utmost care. Intimately prime as your father did
its double jagged sickles and its tight-sprung mouth, arrange
its hidden ribbon of links. Then turn for home, moving
heavily downward into sleep.
Only to dream of iron laughter shouting in the wood
and the spare, insatiable gaze
that will see your own flesh folded in the earth
and then will sit back patient, waiting;
grinning till the wandered, bone-white stars begin to fall.

Drifts

When winter closes on us, then we feel
the first bite of the dark mouths of the dead.

Above the old persuasions of the wind, out of the glimmering night
their voices pile against the windows and the doors,
levelling the contours of the life outside the house
so that neither you nor I
can quite remember
what the world beyond the walls was like.

The tree we knew in summer, when
it thrust its flagrant bunches at the sky, became
a cage of birds, and captured
all our promised heartbeats in its limbs

has shrunk to no more
than a trap of hoisted sticks:
a thing like any other, buried
in the friendly susurration of the snow
that only slowly
brings its weight to bear against the world.

These patient pilings, voice on voice,
will smother us in time, but still
we draw them to our fingers' ends, and still
we marvel at the pure, transfigured message of their symmetry.

A woman of my acquaintance

You said that you were born
into a time of snows. And I believe you.
I have come across your birthplace often
when I tramped the hills in winter;
a place concealed
among the silent corries, drifted
full of quiet blindness and unprinted
with the smallest blemish of a mark of life.

You are like that stone
we tried to raise once from a sodden field.
Thirty hands of men, running with sweat
and splintered to the bone
went coaxing over it. Caressing,
squeezing, beating on its sides
in supplication, still they failed
to rouse the slightest movement from it.

Its roots went deeper than we knew; it moored itself
against the bottomless sorrow of the earth.

So now I warn you to take care.
If any bolt of happiness once threatens you
get up and draw the blinds, extinguish
all the lamps. And settle down
beneath the stairs with your good book.
And hide there till the terror of it passes on.

Finishing the picture

In just the way that words will precede sense
sometimes, linking and stringing themselves together
like an infant dropping beads together on a cord
inscrutably, forming their own singular relationships

till all at once, after
a sudden, momentary pause
a necklace or a poem are seen to come complete,

so, peering through the swollen eyes of a binocular
I saw the stag go down upon its knees in silence
in a spume of blood and hair.
But somehow without meaning, locked
inside a language of its own

until the wind brought to me,
after a tiny hesitation of my heart,
the bitter consummation of the rifle shot.

Drowning among mountains

Now even the hills are lost to view.
Where yesterday they rose before us, waves
of chiming granite, blood-carnelian, glitter
of a sea of mica lights,
today a colourless mist sequesters all that radiance.

This is a mist we know too well.
Its acid on the tongue, its wicked droplets
gathered in the hair, the lashes of the eyes. How
voices swim from us and drown, and how
its bitter moisture soaks through to the bone.

Slowly and heavily,
in air that seeps between our actions and our thoughts
we clamber through the dripping valleys

while somewhere above our heads the summits flash
and call to one another, jewelled and invisible.

Uninvited guests

Rattle the door chains, beat
your cabalistic tattoos on the letterbox, and crowd
the worn linoleum of the landing.
No need to shout, no need
to toll your names like passwords through the door.
I know you all, can register you all
in hard, minutest detail
from your egg-stained waistcoats
to your vast and communal lipstick grin.

Maybe one day I'll let you in
with your acid-green bottles and funereal cigars;
but for the moment I prefer
to sit here quietly in the semi-dark.
Listening to the riot of my own breath
and warming myself before a little fire of words.

Black name

We saw him coming from a long way off,
looking neither
to the right nor to the left,
the last light falling round him.

The moon hung poised.
The fish fled from him, flying
in silver through the streams:
the night wind huddled round the house.

And I believe he would have noticed nothing,
and passed straight by along the road –
so why then did you call out
in your clearest voice
his black name over and over?

Chalybeate spring

As if I stood at last beside
a source of fabulous water, out of which
all new life bubbled upward through the rock.
That was how it was that afternoon
in late Glen Markie.

A font of alabaster quartz, smoothed out
by centuries into a perfect chalice, endlessly discharged
a glittering, spellbound freshet over stones
to spread, and somehow sniff the air,
then rush off down the mountain, teeming with its destinies.

Around me, from the deepest hags
a misty dusk was rising. Brawling choirs of stags
were roaring out their fevers and their lusts
as I strode downwards in the gathering dark.

Feeling that clear liquid running in me,
surging in my blood
until I felt that I could reach, and pluck
the little yellow lights of home
and cradle them like glowing insects in my palm.

Harbingers

A friend once told me how, before
a great outbreak of cholera or yellow
fever struck his father's village into dust,
certain families had seen, outside
their windows or their doors
the figure of an angel trembling in the air at noon.

Its form, each one agreed, was of a beauty
almost beyond speech: a radiant innocence
haloed in chromatic light that seemed to murmur
soundless words of benison and peace.
Nonetheless, within ten days,
the remnants of these families
were broken with exhaustion after burying their dead.

And I recalled a day in August, on the burning moor,
when I watched lean, red dogs that quartered
to the right and to the left
before a straggled line of men.
Their bodies flowed like wine above the heather, every muscle
shaped in the fluidity of oils, each fibre
of their coats a blaze of russet lights.

They trembled as they smelled the nestling coveys.
Wrapped in intense innocence, they ignored
the dark oiled barrels swinging into place,
but floated forward, almost motionless;
the dazzling harbingers of a day of blood.

A memoir from the mind-camp [31]

As I lie here in the oven,
waiting for the whitening fires to start
above this floor of sand which is
the colour of the fabled desert.

So now in the white of my mind I hear
only the old inimitable cadence of her voice.
"There was never anyone I loved like you. No,
never, never anyone like you."

I think of this
and think of how I might have seen her yesterday
with both her hands like raddled maps,
white as a leper's, reaching out for me.

Her face starved into the bone
and all her teeth tucked in some stranger's pocket,
leaving her shrunk gums bare and lurid, squeezed
like skinless fingers in her mouth. Her features
lost and empty, barren as the surface of the moon.

I should have spat on her, had it been yesterday.
I should have tramped
her birdlike skeleton down into the mud:
passed on remorseless, left her
blank and nameless, shuttered in
the featureless horizons of this place.
Rolled into a ball her bleak rags,
thrown them on the fire, and gathered out of them
a small, sustaining heat.

Instead, today, inside the oven
and waiting for the flames to start,
I can think of no more
than my longing for the simple cadence of her voice.
"But there was never anyone I loved like you. No,
never, never again anyone like you."

Poems published in magazines during Ian Abbot's lifetime but not included in *Avoiding the Gods* (1988)

Arranged in chronological order of publication.

Here
beneath
the
moon
the
corn
is
a
white
river
flowing
through
dark
husks
of
trees
while
overhead
the
sharp
stars
cry
out
like
birds.

Here

Here
beneath
the
moon
the
wheat
is
a
white
river
flowing
through
dark
husks
of
trees
while
overhead
the
sharp
stars
cry
out
like
birds.

How important

How important
it is
that in blowing
on this rose
I watch myself
fall in petals
to the floor.

The mine

Too often now
I have arrived at what you seek and fear
and touched it
and have not turned away

but stayed to finger its design
and bring it piecemeal
              burning
to your worlds of sad half-sleep.

It came with a blood wrench
at my first fingering.
The stain dazed then
and I longed to return to those I knew

but now
at the pithead
among the black trees
the moon clings to the mounds of my collection

if she went among her children
she would not go more gently
than she does among these pieces.

Departures

You sat
in the branches of the tree
where you had alighted after your long flight.

The upper air you said
was cruel.
Your flesh froze
to your bones, your eyes glazed, you survived
only by a miracle.

But here;
here the air was an immense glove
that caressed your body
and set your bloodstream humming like a hive.

I listened
and believed every word
and so can sit my time out in this little tree
too old now to learn how to fly.

On that day

On that day
I shall unlock my linens
and unfold my heavy gowns.

When bulls and soldiers loll about the steps
and tear the lawns, make ruins of the groves
and of the dove-house,

when salamanders sink their fires
in shallow ponds,
I shall retire to this patient room
and close the door across its oiled and silent hinge.

And shall not hang my body
from any balcony of gold and laurel-leaves.

On that day
I shall unlock my linens
and unfold my heavy gown.

When bulls and soldiers loll about the steps
and tear the lawns, make ruin of the groves
and of the dove-house,
when salamanders sink their fires
in shallow ponds
I will retire to this patient room
and close the door across its oiled and silent hinge.

and will not hang my body
from any balcony of gold and laurel-leaves.

Waking
in the small hours,
staring into the blackness of the moon,
listen
to the terrible torn cry rising everywhere around you.

It is like the sound
of a dog hunting in his sleep, it holds
the noises of bones,
it is full of the presence
of the dead
and of their whisperings.
It is like the keening of whales in the cold oceans.
It is like the shrieking of ice.

I know
there are crystal labyrinths
in the spaces between the stars
and that the sounds ~~from the earth~~ which rise from the earth
wander among them forever.
So, on these nights, the echoes of your dreams
howl upwards from the darkness and are lost.

Small hours

Waking
in the small hours,
staring into the blackness of the moon,
listen
to the terrible torn cry rising everywhere around you.

It is like the sound
of a dog hunted in his sleep, it holds
the noises of bones,
it is full of the presence
of the dead
and of their whisperings.
It is like the keening of whales in the cold ocean.
It is like the shrieking of ice.

I know
there are crystal labyrinths
in the spaces between the stars
and that the sounds which rise from the earth
wander among them forever.
So, on these nights, the echoes of your dreams
howl upwards from the darkness and are lost.

A resurrected long dead soldier

Here he is at last,
discovered after centuries,
flung down headlong into the sodden peat.
He is a bundle of geometries;
a huddle of lines and angles, hollows
where both his eyes were once and where
his ribs confined the spasms of his heart.

Time has imploded him
into a leather map
of everything we are that lasts: the skin,
the nails, the architecture
of his skull, the tiny perfect jigsaws of his hands and feet.
His brain now
an aggregate of clays;
his heart a faceted, crystalline jewel.

They say
that when we sleep, we imitate the dead:
but certainly the dead
do not evoke the sleeping. His silence
as he hugs the earth is absolute. Only along
the sunken roads which cross
his forehead and his face
can we detect
the distant tramping of the future and the past.

Stalactites

You wander through the caverns of his heart.
On the walls you trace
the patterns of rainbows, full
of delight you roam among stalactites and stalagmites;
your skin holds colours of mother of pearl and gold.

But listen; drop by drop
those needles come together.
Imperceptibly they thicken, clot
to pillars of radiant stone.
Slowly the entrances are growing smaller;
soon there will be
no way in left anymore.

Love in February

Myself,
a corpse,
frozen beneath the earth by those late frosts.
My eyes are blank, my ancient mouth
is filled with shining shards of tin.

Each autumn, now,
a stiffness crawls into the earth,
lower and lower, I feel it come
for weeks before the grass
whitens and breaks under your feet,
before your pink, delighted arms point out
that every tree is glass, that the whole
fragile expanse of sky might shatter down
at the mere raising of your voice.
I know these things.
I smell them here where the earth tightens and grips my
bones.

This lasts
and lasts
and then recedes. Gently my lungs expand,
my nostrils flare, my dead, crossed arms
flutter about the white bone of my chest.
Even here, this casing of winter enters into me.

This is, at once, my great achievement and my greatest loss.
Not to know any more
your pale, resurgent body, not to feel
how every smallest detail of the earth exults.
Here it is quiet and content
I am spared at last the fury and rigours of the spring.

November

Trees
sink down into the earth. In the same way
hopes sink out of the heart and are silent.
These hills today, touched
by that fine, sifted snow,
oppress me with their stones. Into the mind
come crawling roots of heather, briar,
the steaming vegetable heat of leaves, and all
the sheltering debris of October.

Soon the eye of the world will shut, and we will look
through windows of ice at its small, uncertain fire.
It will give no heat, like the hearts
of hedgehogs and of voles it will not appear to move.

We will not be sure
whether it will ever flare again.
We will have forgotten what the world was like.

Spring Equinox

Blades, blades
of grass stiffening in the wind
where leaves flash suddenly like shoals.

Tree limbs shudder, beat
like seas against the blue air.
A thin cry
is rising above the pollen-heads; I listen
to the raw voices of the earth.

Moths at the window

Now, in the dead hours of the night,
the insects hurl themselves against the window-pane.

The rain descends: the surface of the glass becomes
a maze of branching puddles where they falter,
twist, and then subside
into a final apathy. They stay there, glued
against the panes till rot and weather pull them down.

But this is my perspective. Seen
from the darkened lawn, this tiny room
becomes a warm, illimitable cave of light,
vast and irresistible,
where I sit pecking at a few intrusive words.

Outside, the garden fumes into the dark, the stars
go swirling in their fathomless geometries.
My phrases fling themselves against the panes
and falter, twist, and in the end
fall down to similar oblivion.

Only, on both sides of the window hang
the merest traces of the smear of wings.
Moth-dust and word-dust, clinging for a time
until they both are washed away
and only the blank translucence of the glass remains.

Looking with new eyes

He claims that he has parted us at last.
with no more
than a bitter exhalation of his breath,
the simplest gesture of his wrist, he has returned me
the freedom of the air which is my element,

while he attains his own. I watch him
standing on the beach, encumbered
by the poverty of his estate.
A frail and shrunken figure, blinded
by the glitter of his crown
and leaning now upon the staff which injured me.

The thought comes suddenly
that I might move him here as he will move
his old man's blunted mind
and that I held unknowingly,
through all these years,
the sorceries of his heart in my hands.

Keeper and cottage

Every evening since the spring
he has come here,
picking through the litter
and the buried bones of the life that he once had.

Now he finds,
with the awkward stoop from the hips
that we have come to recognise
as his own small triumph
in the incomprehensible wreckage of his house,
such simple items as a kettle,
blackened and bent, the dull blade
of his knife that once
removed the unwilling muscle
from the pale beauty of the bone;
the charred edge of a family photograph.

He clasps these to his chest, wraps them
in the fronds of his ancient jacket. He raises his head,
observes, in the rooms
where his old life now has passed away,
the resurrection of the willow-herb and thistle,
the tiny shooting stars of birch.

He watches in the darkening hills
the onset of autumn, the confusion
of decay. Then turns again
to prowl his memories, inching his way
through the elaborate ruin of the summer.

The comforting word

It begins
with the mouth open, the lips curved
round these first useful vowels, shaped as they are
like the most benign of hillsides
where the bland sheep wander and every tooth is flat.

It progresses
to the scarp of moor and wicked heather
as the red fox tunnels
hour after hour to his complaisant prey.
The first syllabic bloodstains line his jaw.

It ends
on the bleakest granite, the climber
peeking from the quiet stone
and falling as the vowels fall
over and over, till the silent earth receives him
and the cries of his small body vanish in the air.

Climbing through ammonites

Little spirals, scattered on the hills.
A litter of signatures, fastened
on the very soul of stones.

Let you and I move among them
casually, as if we did not hear
their curved, eternal voices
singing in the small bones of our ears.

As if, when we arrange them on the shelves
they will not speak to us
of what we think we have,
of what we think we hold forever.

Of how the sea-bed of one age
rears into the mountains of another.

A mad old woman dying

When that single face behind your face
suddenly burst,
in tears, in ecstasy, in the anguish of certainty
out of its bone-white wrinkled shell,

then it was as if
candles had flared up in your flesh; as if
their warm and multiple radiance
streamed from every age-line, laid
a complex map of light about your eyes,
the keelbone of your nose, around
the pale, reciting borders of your mouth.

It was as if
your final, solitary face,
greedy for joy
had welcomed every other face
you ever knew, or wore,
or gave without regret to this old lover or to that.

They had returned
like little birds
to perch along your cheekbones
and to nest around your hair; chattering
among themselves
about the subject of your latest great adventure in the world.

Speaking in solitary

Here is the quick noise on the pipes.
Here is the base tune patterned out,
the sly word, typed
collectively on basest metal.

Now we have the way in, now we have learned
so finely to articulate
everything we learn about the world
along these little tubes
of intimate material. We have devised
a language of our own that will impart
our deep, inconsequential secrets
out along the lines
to others tuned into our tapping.

But where will it get us in the end, this
small deceit of codes? This beating out of necessary dialect?
No further than the door shut in our faces, and the tramp
of heavy boots across the flags. The hand
that is always outside, tightening the key.

Unknown friends, we are left with no more
than a square of furtive sky, filled with clouds always
colliding in their own tongue:
the real world
speaking to us in a language we have never
come to understand.

Passing through September

Sky cools. The earth
begins imperfectly to whiten
and the first uncertain skeins go wavering south.

Under the distant horns
a man in his solitary shell
is walking among the multiplied hills.
The slopes
have sloughed off summer imperceptibly: so from himself
the veils of another year
are peeling slowly like abandoned skin. Dry grass,
the empty bones of heather,
lies down finally beneath his feet.

His shadow in the low sun
leans backwards from his heels
under a sky of scribbled chevrons, flying
into the bright, receding season,
while step by step he moves
toward his patient, white horizon.

He is walking
into the thin line of the future;
into the numberless rising voices
and the terrible vistas of ice.

Life history

Here by the languid river
young birches have crowded together.
Reddish in spring, in summer silver-green,
in winter printed with the final grey of snow.

How they resemble girls that you and I have known:
the paper skin beneath the bark
that hardens slowly into age-rings,
their sure, bright umber burning into lichen grey.
Still congregating by the river
where a changeless water rolls and rolls away.

Looking for wild men

The forest burns with parakeets, while far below
the muscled river shoulders down its bed. Along the banks,
in shadow-caves and under the flat leaves,
we detect the glitter of jewelled eyes.

We rehearse
uneasy speeches, gestures full
of contrition and of calm intent
which our worn features broadcast to the world.
Swollen with trinkets, our civilised boat
is riding low on the broad river, while on every side
we yearn for the sudden flash of plumes.

Under the immaculate, laundered whites
the mind
is full of the barbarous cries of birds; the currents
of the blood eddy and surge
beneath the calm skin we sail on.
We watch the eyes, and all we lack
is a place where we can put to shore.

But those wild banks are unattainable.
Time passes, till suddenly
the forest is silent and the eyes are gone.
Depressed, we huddle in the boat, our beads
and platitudes all useless at the last.

Poems first published posthumously

An educated rabbit's view of the snare

The universe is no more
than a bubble of soap
caught in the bright wire confines
of a simple frame.
The shape it makes is certain, and occasioned
by what they tell me are the lines of purest form.
That is to say
the universal geometries of least resistance.

How can I comment? All I would like to mention
is that I have come across that one barbaric wire,
that simple loop of universe
inside which the world was coruscating like a rainbow.
Naively, I thought that I might force an entry
and maybe write new chapters in the laws of things.

But what am I left with finally? Only a vision
of the radiant cosmos growing darker, a multitude
of clamorous small sounds ebbing
at the end into an awful, tinny mirth

which is that delicate
soap-bubble, tightening its grin.

Cameraman

You say the poet's task is simply to record,
like the blind lens of a camera,
small scenes out of the world's
careering carnival
and to freeze them without commentary
in the page; like insects shut
in a kind of cellulose amber.

It's possible I could agree with this.
But if I do, who could explain
the sort of camera that I've been fitted with?
What geometry of lens is it
that on one side
can telescope the universe into its eye
one single, floodlit moment;
while on the other, simultaneously,
sends its calm, converging rays
to play minutely through the shuttered places of my heart?

On certain nights

On certain nights,
inexplicable tides
seem to set the earth rocking like a shell.

Raise it to your ear then
and you will hear that distant roar
which is like the beating of an immense sea;
but fainter still,
so faint that you may not be sure
whether you have heard them at all,
you will catch
a perfect succession of limpid notes,
a few strains of a rare and everlasting dance.

Then the dance will go on in your head forever,
leaving you dissatisfied
and ill at ease with the world.

Musteline

This is the one who, clothed
in her bright body hair will yield
her supple backbone like a carter's whip.

This is the one
who tirelessly will run you down, and show you
what it means always to have her blonde curve at your hip.

This is the one that you have all your life been frightened of.
The one who will transfix you,
steal you with her scent,
and print her perfect, bloody muzzle on your lip.

A real death

Behind a pane of curving glass,
under a rudely-painted desert sun
the python stacks his Shiraz coils on rock.

His head is sunk
in the tight, volcanic well of his body.
and as the crowd, transfixed,
stares at the essence of that painted stillness,
the sun
deploys imagined rays
about the limitless vistas of the cage: the snake
becomes one with the desert stones and nothing moves
that the crowd does not move there in imagination.
The patterning of insects, swirls
of overheated air, a slow pulse
beating in the body of the snake.

Until a flap slides open and a rat, alive,
is let loose in the cage.
Its pink feet whisper in the sand, its nose
is raised to sniff the air; while out of the sombre
well of coils his blunt head floats: eyes
lidless and fixed, the tongue
that tastes the air, the jaw
a long, unshakeable grin.

Held in a cage
within a cage the rat, transfixed, lies down.
And out of the placid, painted scene,
leisurely and real,
the slow uncoilings come.

The poetry of television

In the brittle light of midday
the corpses are arranged along the street.
Already, side by side, their devastated grins
are soaring upwards, flying
at a sky still trembling with the final shards of noise.

While here,
replete and lounging by the fire,
we juggle earnest, empty theories around the room

and notice how only the naked feet recall
a ruined field of silent, landed butterflies.

Landscapes

Evening.
The grey road mapped with ice,
scarred with hollows and pools.

The sky
is green-blue, transparent.
Along the horizon
a red flush lights the snowfields:
rows of black trees
stitch the sky against the earth.

I feel that I am passing
from a point to a point within a picture,
Icarus falling.
The centre of one world,
unnoticed in the corner of the other.

The omnibus

The omnibus stopped the street.
It rolled up
to the crossing
and the morning's traffic parted
and grew many arms
and waved it through.

MICHELIN glowed on its sides
above wheels
spoked in yellow
and
Ballymena to Strasbourg
on an open stair
winding to green leather seats.

As it passed
the street was wide
and crowded with round faces,
it was the morning a war had ended
and if I'd a hat
I'd have tossed it high
into the brightening air.

Starlings

Somewhere very distant, and who knows
how many years ago,
the walls of a great mosque
fell sliding suddenly into the sand.

Immense tiled walls, glazed walls
where were labyrinths
of intricate, metallic blue and green,
oil-purple, veined
with topaz, alizarin, fathomless black.
Indecipherable, incomparable walls,
they fell with a sound
like the rushing of numberless wings.

And now
by some mysterious process,
several splinters from those walls
have animated themselves here in my garden.
Razor-edged and busy, they attempt
to resurrect that fabulous memory of their past.
One matches his patterns to another's, studies the result
and scintillates into the air, exploding with frustration.
He scatters crumbs of dusty bread like alms.

A summer engagement

Trapped in the net
of his own vanity
Custer stands in the midst of his dead heroes,
his six-guns crackling uselessly at air.

But after a time we find him
heaped with the other usual corpses,
his glorious scalp stripped raw

while his conqueror staggers from the field,
the golden, bloodied hair
bounds at her hip like an animal.

How I forgot

How I forgot
when we parted
the wild geese clamoured
in a sky blanched to the colour of bone.

For such a long time, it seemed,
the bright seasons blustered through their carnival,
riotous with potency and grief.

But the blood slows
with an infinite stealth
the heart's leaves turn and fall,
till, suddenly you are no longer here
and the crooked birds
sound their warnings
and the first frosts
are waiting on the grass.

Throughout the green night

Throughout the green night,
under the eye of the moon at its apex,
the vivid cries of the dead ignite like flares
and while the last smoke
hesitates from chimneys,
someone is intoning over and over again into the dark
the name of a woman,
a child,
the name of a lost dog.

He caught me by the roadside

He caught me by the roadside
in the half-light, uncoiling his long body
from the waiting ditch
and stretching his dark limbs against the dusk,
while he slithered his gaze over me
in a trap of eels.

His voice, it seemed,
moved into me unaided, whispers asked,
"Now did you meet a dog about you on the road?
A long white dog with just
a brown place on him, somewhere and again?
A dog that runs all night, and with a nose
that smells out children in their little beds?"

Unpublished poems [32]

IAN ABBOT.

I seem
to see you
walking
under the elms
in this rainy autumn
and the day
for you
is
as mine is

grey
brown
broken yellow of wet leaves –
rude
with impatience
of waiting for winter.

it seems
that little has changed
for you go quickly
as I do
laying dark footprints
between the brittle trees

and the leaves
which blow about you
like shot birds
also
browse down
round my shoulders

but
they
tumble
too

where my lover waits
at the tree's edge

and I find
that you
have long ago
faded from days
that turn
now
on a new plane.

Ian R. M. Abbot
27·10·67

I seem 33

I seem
to see you
walking
under the elms
in this rainy autumn
and the day
for you
is
as mine is

grey
brown
broken yellow of wet leaves –
rude
with impatience
of waiting for winter.

It seems
that little has changed
for you go quickly
as I do
laying dark footprints
between the brittle trees

and the leaves
which blow about you
like shot birds
also
blow down
round my shoulders

but
they
tumble
too

where my lover waits
at the tree's edge

and I find
that you
have long ago
faded from days
that turn
now
on a new plane.

From Frances and Ian
To Hilary
Christmas, 1967
With love.

    Cold
           In the hard weather
    We may
        Make
    For each other —

    You
        Are a warm night
    That we
        Both
    May walk in.

To Hilary [34]

C<small>OLD</small>
   I<small>N THE HARD WEATHER</small>
W<small>E MAY</small>
   M<small>AKE</small>
F<small>OR EACH OTHER</small> —

Y<small>OU</small>
   A<small>RE A WARM NIGHT</small>
T<small>HAT WE</small>
   B<small>OTH</small>
M<small>AY WALK IN</small>.

After the Equinox

This is a threadbare season, when the plundered trees
dangle the remnants of their rags
in a limp, exhausted silence.

Invisible all summer, gradually the hills
insinuate themselves
behind the thinning branches, while distant cries of shepherds
hurrying off their sides
puff out into the air like small explosions.

This is a waiting season, caught
in a hushed bubble of expectancy

and speaking to me
of those past times when, curled in bed
I used to hold my breath
until my young head burned, trying and trying to prevent
the awful, creeping advent of the dark.

Raptor

Like that small bird
feathered and beaked in metal, scintillant;
like one bird livid
with furious colour, trembling
from wing-tip to wing-tip, and held
on fierce strings
quite unmoving in the endless air,
so a single notion moves its glare across the soft map of the mind.

The harmless alphabets prostrate themselves
suppliant and breathless, waiting
as the half-imagined shadow hovers overhead;
and hangs, and in a single, soundless moment
falls and strikes and fixes its difficult barbs.

Then rises and soars away. Leaving the mind
among a carnage of phrases, smeared
with words and the colour of words.
and the poem torn into being.

White hands, slender

white hands, slender
and skilled
and boned like birds
adjust the lamps
and dim this little room of unborn things.

Their shadows roam across the walls,
across your skin, across
the sleeping corners of your face.

Outside
the world is dark,
the streets are full of quiet cries,
but here the hands drift down
and down
and downward always

with inviolable calms.

The retired soldier's lesson

His mind, I felt, was a concentric castle, fortified
like those I dreamed about
in great Arthurian tales when I was young.
It had, across the years,
repelled the thrusts of legions of invaders, and earned him
a lasting name for dourness in the district.

So, meeting him by accident
one evening in the small bar of a small hotel, I thought
I might attempt the feat myself.
I measured out my ordnance with precision
and slowly, armed with magazines and arsenals of drams,
settled myself for a long and difficult siege.

The outer curtain-wall was easy, crossed
on scaling-nets of chatter he let down himself,
and inside it
we wandered for a long time over lawns of conversation
delicately laid, and quiet,
and affectionately tended over years.

But I noticed how, whenever we approached
the inner wall, a certain wariness possessed him. Lack of ease
would take him now and then behind his stones, to narrowly
regard me through embrasures.
I began to hear
the almost-silent clicks of cross-bows cocking.

But I pressed on, through into the killing-ground
where each step became murderous. I stumbled
into great debating pits he opened up before me. Vast, truculent
machineries of argument were rolled up across my path
and finally
a warning flight of quarrels whizzed towards my head.

Then he was gone completely. His lips still moved
but I could feel him off somewhere
inside his private keep, preparing vats
of boiling oils and pitch, his great door bolted shut.
My nerves had all deserted me. I retired politely,
broke camp, and hauled my baggage-train onto the long road home.

When we meet now we talk without formality, but with
the fine reserve of ancient combatants. I should have liked
to cross the threshold, have him conduct me
through the mysteries of his apartments. But in all the years
I've lived here
no-one I've run into yet has managed that.

Tumour

You are here you are
moving, you are
breathing and the pure
light of you gilds the walls. I myself slide
just at the edge of your corona
from room to room, my eyes suspicious,
ceaselessly probing
the blackest corners of the house.

I know that I am going
where I know that you will never go. There
where in the velvet of uncounted evenings
a thickness spreads across
the speaking portions of the tongue and shoots
its shadowed secondaries
blackly upwards on their hawsers to the head.

Everything fails in time. The body every minute slowly,
slowly winds down into dark. I tell you
I am watching for it ceaselessly
in the very way that I attended
just that single moment when the light failed into dusk
and we agreed the evening had come down.

Now my mouth is riddled by your nebulae, obscured
by clouds of shadowed dust. I want no more
than to stare along those ropes that moor you to myself.
To gaze into your gilded centre, blind with light
of promises. And down into
that place in you where all my words
tomorrow might rise newly made.

Omens

One midnight,
Above the hill,
A star
Touched the treetops,
Dulled
And set.

Along the silent river,
The creak and beat of rowlocks
Passed
Into the darkness ......

Thus you came,
Like a star,
Like men rowing;
But the star set,
And the boat passed
Into the silence.

Omens

One midnight
above the hill,
a star
touched the treetops,
dulled
and set.

Along the silent river,
the creak and beat of rowlocks
passed
into the darkness.

Thus you came,
like a star,
like men rowing;
but the star set,
and the boat passed
into the silence.

Khamsin

Mother
of the scimitar, wind that comes down like a scythe,
suddenly I saw your eyes above me in a sulphurous dawn.

Your love-breath roared around my life,
charmed open all my veins.
Quietly the freshets of my blood deserted me.

But as you ran contented fingers
through the grains of my dry sand,
you do not see
how the scorpion's heart-shaped trigger rises in the shade.

Mykonos

The windmill's sails revolve
under an immense weight of falling light.

Along the shore
cicadas are crying, horses
wander patiently along empty streets
and night after night
the hot wind
burns us away to a brittle ash.

Only in the morning
waking over and over by this clamorous sea
do we hear again
the faintest echoes of familiar dreams.

A.M. alphabet

In these early hours
language is moving through the circle of the lamp.
Stones whisper quiet litanies: the deepest
murmuring of granite, and rolling voices
singing in the belly of the stream.

The garden branches; every phrase
extends its curious shoots
and, word on glimmering word
slowly the morning composes itself

till suddenly the dawn comes like the turning of a page:
completes the world.
The poem a brief cacophony of birds.

Evening

Tide of the light, receding,
a sediment of pale stars
left on a darkening beach
and the earth a froth-bubble
dancing
on the edge of unguessable deeps.

Plain of jars

From the depths of the fire the voices rise.
Out of the fire's archaic depths
the little roses rise.
Struggle forward, reach for them, and die.

Under revolving fastnesses of stars,
the moon's poised, icy hammer,
the body of the earth is bone
a few cold, fretting words
that pass and pass
from one ravaged night into another.

Returning

In tides that draw the deep colds in
small waves break in the depths of our hair –
the sea is raising its old ache.

We see
that the lights cry out and are doused
the shoreline flattens
and slowly
a pureness drifts into the dark

till only the faces of our mothers shine,
hung in weak knots above the beach.

THE MAGII IN SOLITUDE

Old men in winter
under a cold moon
moving across the snows

dreams sleeping in us
like wine
in the mind's dark stone
while the sharpness in air and stars
blackens
the brittle payhs of travel
through an empty land.

The purity of snow
is terrible

a mind laid open by the wind
that hones all ⟨xxxxx⟩
to a silent cry
shrinks from the infinity of this empty night
where the frost burns down
to the bone's cold fire.

And still no murmered end
breaks on this solitude
of we who have come beyond grief

for on such nights
the world
is given over to this endless journeying
towards what lonely place

—each sound shut off beneath the earth
and the still air shaken, emptied of its wings.

The magi in solitude

Old men in winter
under a cold moon
moving across the snows

dreams sleeping in us
like wine
in the wind's dark store
while the sharpness in air and stars
blackens
the brittle paths of travel
through an empty land.

The purity of snow
is terrible

a mind laid open by the wind
that hones all
to a silent cry
shrinks from the infinity of this empty night
where the frost burns down
to the bone's cold fire.

And still no murmured end
breaks on the solitude
of we who have come beyond grief

for on such nights
the world
is given over to this endless journeying
towards what lonely plane –

each sound shut off beneath the earth
and the still air shaken, emptied of its wings.

Prayer to the god of the mine

You who have become
the red eye at the centre of the fire,
the immaculate barb from which depends
the slow and measured rising of the heron
out of its labyrinth of streams,

you who are
the forge at the heart of iron.
Do not lead me down
harnessed and unaided into all this pathless black.

Give me at least a little light,
the merest cooling ember – and no more
than the whispered rumour of a wing
that might, despite all, bear me up.

And if these fail, then at the last
a hammer I can strike against the walls.
To set them ringing, shouting
with the echoes of my lost, familiar voice.

Thoughts after the funeral, for W.

Only darkness here,
    only darkness,

filling the hollows of conscience
lying in the mind
suppressing memories
that struggle upwards
in a fierce drowning
through translucent vales of water
to the light.
                Some shadows fly:
                slip from the lids
                to burst on the surface
                like petals
                thrown suddenly on snow
                but these are small things
                chiming in valleys
                so far off
                that their bells din dumb.
                Leave them
                there is no pain there.

Dreams in the evening

And the earth turns in its sleep.
A gold haze spreads over the corn, along
the broken wall where the adders lie.
You caress
their dark diagonals, their arrow heads
pressed flat against the sand
the immense heat presses down.

And caught up in this red light
the river drains down into its bed,
the sky
is running away, the sound
of late bells drifts like smoke –

across the corner of the field
where that remorseless dog goes running
evening after evening
in a straight line towards the horizon.
His tongue hangs from his mouth like meat
and the scent of him is in the air
for a long time after he is gone.

Writing late

Night creaks by outside the window.
Time is freezing in the farthest stars,
in numberless cups of coffee, in the smoke from cigarettes.

But the page remains awake always.
With its wide eyes open
and its blank grin stretching on and on.

Retrospective premonitions

We look down at the raw wounds in the earth.
And after a long time, after
what seems an eternity
of listening to the strains
of a far-off martial music,
of scanning the horizons
for banners of inevitable smoke,
then we walk forward, step off the edge
and fold ourselves contentedly in the dark ground.

Perhaps, after all, those tunes
were no more than the distant lift of conversations.
Perhaps the smoke
is rising yet from fat, domestic chimneys.
Still, we lie down solemn and placid, waiting
while the soil is shovelled on our heads.

And no-one has tricked us here, no-one has paid us.
No-one has led us to the edge and pushed us in.
We dug these graves ourselves
when we were children; dug down in the dead past
laughing and full of whispers:
innocently nibbling at the earth
there is that old time when the very air was milk.

Unpublished notebook or draft poems from the archive 35

Along the wall the heads look down

Along the wall the heads look down.
They are the remnants
of the famous of another time.
From Rome, from Greece, Byzantium,
they gaze now in an awful, leprous melancholy.
Time has smoothed their features as the tide blurs stones.

This
is how we see each other, and
to tell the truth, the only way we have
of looking at ourselves.
The perfect details that we were dissolved,
whole areas
of mind and body bled away
in the slow, continuous acid rain.
We are left
with only what we are on any certain day:
remnants looking out
at other remnants
of what an hour ago we thought imperishable.

Within me

Within me
the grubs are fattening, sleek
and yellow
waiting for that time
when they will make their exits
through my sides.

And I will flower then,
yellow and shining
until they leave me
drilled and empty
in a rotting wind.

Then I will dance from my station
like a husk of crow.

River of deep winter, when the ice

River of deep winter, when the ice
that locks your stiff reeds
holds a blank sky
that is not my own
then the knife of exile turns
and turns upon the presence of remembered kings
and rising sorrow breaks in me
your dark winter flood.

Here is where

Here is where
the year expires in blood;
its blood banners
flung into the harsh north-westerlies. The wind
that strips the russets into blackened twigs.

The wind
that strips you now
of all your hues of girlhood: all
the solemn colours of your marriage blown
into a little hurl of leaves, a little
cluttered radiance.

Somewhere in the forest at my door
a creature is padding round the traps,
nosing them out, and curling
his long lip at the smell of iron.

History rolls away

History rolls away,
carried on the round lumber of skulls.
A name might surface here and there.
A face shine out, a white hand
vainly waving
at some familiar, hoped for help.
Years later, the slightest possessions
are found lying by the side of the road.
Who knows where they came from?

I know that somewhere

I know that somewhere
in a yard of hammers, in a ruin
of blood and bone
a part of me sits and listens
and will not come home.

Three words, no more

Three words, no more
falling from a sky whose beauty
no-one suspects, whose dirty clouds
might seem to swell with nothing more than snow.

They flutter down in silence, come to rest
on eyelids and on lips, and shape themselves
precisely to the contours of your life.
Time freezes in them and endures
like thickened water under ice,

so when at last you move, and speak, commit
them all to vapour with your breath,
your voice
is the voice of an old man, sour and alone
raging at the lovers in the street.

Here in September

Here in September
these leaves I raised once to my lips
have turned to corruption like small and intricate tongues

The innocent greens of summer, and all
their patient intimacies, gathered
from the fluids of the earth
and pumped colossally from blanched roots out
to tiny, foetal, barely-visible veins

seem all at once to be reduced
to spectacles of red mouths hanging from the twigs.

The wormed fruits moulder on the ground. Beneath
their bold skins
coloured like the coats of ancient soldiers,
the thin, blind grubs are working, fattening
through labyrinths of rot.

I hold you here
you red leaves; burnished apples
picked out of the dying lawn.
My own white flesh is riddled
through with intimations of decay. Year after year
the merciless seasons plunder me, reduce
my own tongue
to a dry, red flapping leaf that in the end
will spiral down to silence.

No matter. Under the enormous, patient
carapace of frost

[incomplete]

Here in September
these leaves I raised to my lips
have turned to corruption like small and intricate tongues.

The innocent greens of summer, and all
their patient intimacies, gathered
from the fluids of the earth
and pumped colossally from blanched roots out
to tiny, foetal, barely-visible veins

seem all at once to be reduced
to spectacles of red tongues hanging from the twigs.

The wormed fruits moulder on the ground. Beneath
their bold skins,
coloured like the coats of ancient soldiers,
the thin, blind grubs are working, fattening
through labyrinths of rot.

I hold you here
you red leaves; burnished apples
picked out of the dying lawn.
My own white flesh is riddled
through with intimations of decay. Year after year
the merciless seasons plunder me, reduce
my own tongue
to a dry, red flapping leaf that in the end
will spiral down to silence.

No matter. Under the enormous, patient
carapace of frost

Death in the rose.

Ringed with dark sand
wide
shingles of crimson

and
here
with velvet for lips and tongue
is the stain and taste

the
slow
music
of red
of darkening
      wine

Death in the rose

Ringed with dark sand
wide
shingles of crimson

and
here
with velvet for lips and tongue
is the stain and taste

the
slow
music
of red
of darkening
              wine

You will say

You will say
that there is nothing
in the coming of the dark,
the moon
like a barb, odours
of blood among the pines.

But I say
that the twilight eats away my heart
and that your hands,
pale and lustrous,
peacefully asleep,
speak loudest of the labyrinths
that gather between now and the morning.

Trees

Trees
stand
in a green cage
of wind
and

an old woman
passes among
them
unaware

of weak leaves
hurled
to her heavy
back
and to the road's
wet tar.

The wind blows

The wind blows
about the dumb feet of the dead.
Out of the clear air, above
the plain configurations of your voice
a single, constant voice reiterates
its single, simple word.

After the death of the body
nothing else is left that we can move
into the dominion of the mind, the pure imagination.

In my veins the pack is running

In my veins the pack is running.
My limbs are thin, worn weary
from all this baying and the call of blood.
Around the silent rooms
from door to door
my body wanders, sniffing at the air.

Outside the moon is burning:
here the shadows swarm
above the bed where your hair
drenched the pillow.

And in my sleep, in quiet
corners of this dreaming house
unnumbered feet are running,
running.

Ian Abbot (1947-1989)

Notes

Introduction

1 From an obituary of Ian Abbot written by Joy Hendry in Acc. 12737/20 in NLS.
2 Hutchison, Alexander. 'Remembering Ian Abbot' in Hendry, Joy (ed.) *Chapman 102-103*. 2003. 99-101: 100.
3 Montgomerie, William. 'Ian Abbot' in *Scottish Poetry Library Newsletter, No. 14, Feb. 1990*.
4 Montgomerie, William. Letter of 22/19/1989 to Frances Abbot. Acc. 12737/20. NLS.
5 Hutchison, Alexander. 'Remembering Ian Abbot' in Hendry, Joy (ed.) *Chapman 102-103*. 2003. 99-101: 99.
6 McManus, Tony. 'Avoiding Gods and Bending Ears' in *Cencrastus 29*. 1988. 29.
7 Anonymous. *The Edinburgh Review No. 82*. 1988.
8 http://www.heraldscotland.com/sport/spl/aberdeen/poet-takes-his-secret-to-grave-1.606793
9 Nicholson, Colin in Acc.12737/9, National Library of Scotland.
10 Nicholson, Colin. 'A Kind of Logic' in *Poem, Purpose and Place: Shaping Identity in Contemporary Scottish Verse*. Edinburgh: Polygon. 1992. 238-245: 243.
11 McManus, Tony. 'Avoiding Gods and Bending Ears' in *Cencrastus 29*. 1988. 29.
12 Abbot, Ian. *Avoiding the Gods. Memorial Special Edition*. Edinburgh: Chapman Publishing, 1999.
13 Nicholson, Colin in Acc.12737/9, National Library of Scotland.
14 Fulton, Graham in *Perthshire Advertiser* review of *Avoiding the Gods*. 10/06/1988.
15 In letter to editor of *Short Stories Magazine* Abbot provides a short biographical statement. Nov. 1981 Acc. 12737/15. NLS.
16 Abbot, Ian. 'Scottish Arts Council bursary application' for June 1985 in MS/Morgan DA/1. Acc. 4848/33. (Edwin Morgan's correspondence) in Glasgow University Library.

17 Hutchison, Alexander. 'Remembering Ian Abbot' in Hendry, Joy (ed.) *Chapman 102-103*. 2003. 99-101: 99.
18 Morgan, Edwin. 'Reference:13-6-1985' in MS/Morgan DA/1. Acc. 4848/33. (Edwin Morgan's correspondence) in Glasgow University Library.
19 Acc. 12737/15. NLS.
20 Acc. 12737/17. NLS
21 Acc. 11978/5. *Chapman* papers relating to Ian Abbot.
22 Morgan, Edwin. In a letter dated 25/04/1990 to Joy Hendry. Acc. 11978/5. NLS.
23 Nicholson, Colin. 'Ian Abbot' in *Scottish Poetry Library Newsletter, No. 14, Feb. 1990*.
24 Nicholson, Colin in a letter to Ian Abbot dated 12/12/1985. Acc. 12737/20. NLS.

Avoiding the Gods

25 *Avoiding the Gods* was Ian Abbot's only collection, published in 1988 by Chapman Publishing, Edinburgh. The original acknowledgements read: 'Some of these poems have appeared in *The Arts Review of New South Wales, Cencrastus, Chapman, Lines Review* and *Kayak*.'
26 In Colin Nicholson's part interview and essay on Abbot's work 'A Kind of Logic' he quotes Abbot as saying: "I'm urban by upbringing, come from the city: the country I never knew terribly well until I was in my late twenties. I'd never seen a landscape like this; and not just never seen it, never lived in it. That poem 'Landscape of a highland gentleman', for instance; people really are shaped in that way. It's hard, it's difficult, it's solid and the people in Whitebridge grow out of it, you know, directly. Pretensions disappear; they're straight-forward. Everybody up there responds to it. I just happen to respond in a way which produces poems. It's become such a part of my life that I don't even know when I'm doing it. And sometimes I only realise it's winter when I've written a poem that has that feeling in it." (241)
27 Colin Nicholson claims, in 'A Kind of Logic' that this poem 'combines memories of his (Abbot's) own attempts at silversmithing with earlier political experiences (Abbot had been active in left-wing politics after leaving school). (241)
28 In conversation with Colin Nicholson, Ian Abbot claimed that: "In the wintertime you get a lot of snow (in Whitebridge); you really are forced in on each other and the flaws, if any, in your relationship are laid bare. Memories and other sorts of things which you bring up under such conditions start to grate: they put more pressure on

your relationship, which gradually gets buried under the weight of snow like branches which start to break, and then things begin to fall apart." (241)
29 Abbot claimed, in 'A Kind of Logic' that this poem 'grew out of an error'. "I made a blunder about it which Norman MacCaig once corrected. I thought it was trout that have these thumbnails on their bodies, you know, little whorls to see. He said no, it was something else – I forget what sort of fish it was now. These marks look like wax-resist imprints or paintings and I thought how almost invisible they are, though you can see them if you look for them. Then, I thought that this is the way that people leave traces of themselves on others they meet. The poem is about my inability to leave these traces on the people I meet." (242).
30 *The Glasgow Herald* (20/10/1989) claimed that this poem was based on a real sighting by Abbot in the village of Whitebridge where he lived but that he 'refused to reveal' the woman's identity, thus taking the 'secret to his grave'.
31 In Colin Nicholson's 'A Kind of Logic', he quotes Abbot as having discovered that his Grandmother was Jewish. In this poem Abbot claimed to be 'speaking to roots I'm not aware of having but I know are there' (242).

Poems Published in Abbot's Lifetime

Publication dates can be found in the Bibliography

Poems Published Posthumously

Publication dates can be found in the Bibliography

Unpublished poems

32 With the exception of the poems 'I seem' and 'To Hilary', these are drawn from the Ian Abbot archives in the National Library of Scotland, Acc. 12737/2-13.
33 This poem was typewritten by Abbot, signed and dated 27/10/1967, making it one of his earliest surviving poems. It was given by Abbot to Hilary Kundu, a university friend during the later 1960s. Both Ian and Frances Abbot spent time with Kundu both in Dundee and at University in Edinburgh. Kundu remembers this time as fun, productive and challenging and that Abbot's poems decorated the walls of her room.
34 This poem is dated 'Christmas 1967' and is a gift 'with love' from Frances and Ian Abbot to Hilary Kundu.

Notebook or draft poems from the archive

35 These notebook or draft poems, with the exceptions of 'Here in September' and 'Death in the rose' from the papers of Hilary Kundu, have all been drawn from the Ian Abbot archive in the National Library of Scotland, Acc. 12737/2-13. Most of these poems are untitled, so the first line is used in lieu of a title.

Select Bibliography

Note: while this list is thorough, it is not exhaustive and is mainly to give a sense of how and where Abbot's poems were published, discussed and broadcast.

Book collections

Avoiding the Gods. Edinburgh: Chapman, 1988.
Avoiding the Gods: Memorial Special Edition. Edinburgh: Chapman, 1999.
Finishing the Picture: The Collected Poems of Ian Abbot. Edinburgh: Kennedy & Boyd, 2015.

As editor

School of Poets Calendar. Edinburgh: The Scottish Poetry Library, 1985.

Appearances in anthologies

Poem: 'Speaking in solitary' In: Shaw, Brenda (ed.) *Seagate II*. Durham: Taxus Press, 1984.
Poem: 'Drowning among mountains' In: Berry, Martyn & Brown, Hamish (eds.) *Speak to the Hills: An Anthology of Twentieth Century British and Irish Mountain Poetry*. Aberdeen: Aberdeen University Press, 1985.
Poem: 'Marriages' (for January). In: *School of Scottish Poets Calendar 1986*, edited by Valerie Gillies.
Eight poems: 'Ferns like poems', 'Ariel', 'Ewe against the fence', 'Last dip of the year', 'Finishing the picture', 'Uninvited guests', 'Black name' and 'Ga-Cridhe' In: Glen, Duncan (ed.) *Twenty of the Best [and one more for good measure]: A Galliard Anthology of Contemporary Scottish Poetry*. Edinburgh: Galliard, 1990
Poem: 'The mechanisms of the gin' In: Dunn, Douglas (ed.) *The Faber Book of Twentieth Century Scottish Poetry*. London: Faber & Faber, 1992 (reprinted multiple times).

Seven poems: 'The bestiary of Cortes', 'Ariel', 'A crofter buried', 'Avoiding the gods', 'Shrapnel', 'Ga-Cridhe', 'Harbingers'. In: McCordick, David (ed.) *Scottish Literature in the Twentieth Century: An Anthology*. Aberdeen: Scottish Cultural Press, 2002.

Short story publications

Short story: 'Conquistador' In: Nelson, Michael (ed.) *Short Stories Magazine Vol. 2, No. 3.* February 1982.

Poems in magazines

Three poems: 'Ward seven – December', 'Here' and 'How important' In: *Kayak 15*. San Francisco, 1968.
Poem: 'The mine' In: *George Square Poetry No. 2*. Edinburgh, Edinburgh University Student Publications Board, 1969.
Five poems: 'Sloughing', 'Departures', 'Black name', 'Laurel bush' and 'Montezuma' In: *Lines Review 72*. Edinburgh, March 1980.
Two poems: 'On that day' and 'Small hours' In: *Cencrastus 2*. Edinburgh, Spring 1980.
Ten poems: 'The bestiary of Cortes', 'Shadow-wolf', 'Brain coral', 'Fever', 'Ward seven – December', 'A search for lodgings', 'Landscape of a Highland gentleman', 'Spoor', 'Ariel' and 'A resurrected long dead soldier' In: *Lines Review 77*. Edinburgh, June 1981.
Nine poems: 'Exile', 'Forms', 'Last entry of a polar explorer', 'Stalactites', 'Marriages', 'Spring Equinox', 'November', 'Promenaders on the tideline' and 'Love in February' In: *Lines Review 78*. Edinburgh, September 1981.
Five poems: 'Forms', 'Departures', 'Black name', 'Laurel bush' and 'Montezuma' In: *Chapman 31*. Edinburgh, Winter 1981/1982.
Ten poems: 'An inland sea', 'Wax resist', 'Quiet evenings at home', 'Moths at the window', 'Looking with new eyes', 'Keeper and cottage', Before the flood', 'The comforting word', 'Hephaestus preaching' and 'Drowning among mountains' In: *Lines Review 80*. Edinburgh, March 1982.
Two poems: 'Climbing through ammonites' and 'Mad old woman dying' In: *Lines Review 84*. Edinburgh, March 1983.
Seven poems: 'Ga-Cridhe', 'Bird's eye view', 'Life-line', 'A crofter buried', 'Life history', 'Looking for wild men' and 'Passing through September' In: *Lines Review 93*. Edinburgh, June 1985.
Eight poems: 'A memoir from the mind camp', 'Caliban rising', 'A body of work', 'Vestal', 'Shrapnel', 'The Astrologer', 'Ewe against the fence' and 'A late note to my mother' In: *Rubicon 10*. Canada, Fall 1988.

Poem: 'Drowning among mountains' In: *Lines Review 120*. Edinburgh, March 1992.

Poem: 'A memoir from the mind camp' In: *Faultlines 1*. Inverness, 1992.

Eleven poems: 'An educated rabbit's view of the snare', 'Cameraman', 'Passing through September', 'On certain nights', 'Climbing through ammonites', 'Stalactites', 'Musteline', 'A real death', 'Poetry of TV', 'Landscapes' and 'A resurrected long-dead soldier' In: *Chapman 102-103*. Edinburgh, 2003.

Three poems: 'Climbing through ammonites', 'On that day', 'Passing through September' In: *Northwords Now 24*. Summer 2013.

Four poems: 'The mine', 'How I forgot', 'He caught me by the roadside' and 'Throughout the green night' In: *The Next Review: Vol.2 / Issue 4*. Spring 2015.

Three poems: 'A summer engagement', 'The omnibus' and 'Starlings' In: *The Dark Horse 34*. Summer 2015.

Prizes and awards

For the poem 'Ariel': First prize (of £50) in 1982 Royal Lyceum Theatre Club Poetry Competition.

For the poem 'Scott's first voyage': Second prize (of £35) in the 1985 Scottish Association for the Speaking of Verse / Diamond Jubilee Poetry Competition.

Scottish Arts Council bursary for 1987 (value of £3000).

Shortlist for Saltire Prize for best first book, 1988.

Broadcasting and television appearances

George Bruce recites a selection of Abbot's early poems on BBC's *Scottish Life and Letters* during a broadcast on young writers (c.1969).

Recorded work/ poems for the Scottish Heritage Society, Edinburgh. August 1984.

Recorded work for Broadcasting Corporation of New South Wales. April / May 1985.

Appearance on *In Verse* for STV in 1989. Abbot reads and discusses four of his poems: 'The mechanisms of the gin', 'Ariel', 'Ewe against the fence' and 'Drowning among mountains'.

A reading of 'Crossing the ford' featured in the programme 'Viewpoint' on 05/02/1990.

Archive material

Ian Abbot papers, National Library of Scotland. Acc. 12737 Nos. 1-27. Archive contains poems, drafts, correspondence and other ephemera. Deposited in 2007 by Frances Abbot.

Edwin Morgan correspondence with Ian Abbot, Glasgow University Library, Special Collections. MS Morgan DA/1, Acc. 4848/33. 1 folder.

Editorial correspondence and related papers of *Chapman*. National Library of Scotland, Acc. 11978/ Box. 5: material relating to the publication of Abbot's *Avoiding the Gods*. 1 envelope of material.

Audio tape recording 'Ian Abbot, Dante Jack Clegg and Harvey Holton read at the Christopher North House Hotel, Edinburgh, 28/07/1987. Unpublished sound recording by The Scottish of Scottish Studies.

Obituaries for Ian Abbot

Anon: Obituary notice for Ian Abbot in *The Courier*. 20/10/1989.
Anon: 'Poet takes his secret to grave' in *The Herald*. 20/10/1989.
Anon: 'Poet killed in road accident near his home' in *The Scotsman*. 20/10/1989.
Hutchison, Alexander; Montgomerie, William & Nicholson, Colin: 'Three Appreciations' In: *Scottish Poetry Library Newsletter, No. 14*. February 1990.

Poems for or about Ian Abbot

Yoshimasu, Gōzō. *(trans.)* 'Road'. A poem written in Japanese, dedicated to Ian Abbot and translated by the author in an undated letter to Frances Abbot (c.1989/1990). Note: Yoshimasu's 1989 book *Scotland Diaries* (Tokyo, Shoshi Yamada) contains tributes to Ian Abbot, one of Yoshimasu's hosts during his 1987 visit to Scotland. In a 1989/1990 letter of Yoshimasu to Frances Abbot, he pays tribute to Abbot's 'depth of fire to his mind' and his 'pure beautiful lies'.

Hutchison, Alexander. 'The Hat' In: *Sparks in the Dark*. Akros, 2002, p.16
Hutchison, Alexander. 'The Holt' and 'The Hat' In: *Chapman 102-103*, 2003.

Articles written about Ian Abbot

Berry, Simon (1988) 'Title Fight for Scottish Talent' In: *The Scotsman*. October, 1988. Note: this is coverage for the 'Scottish Best First Book of the Year' and includes two paragraphs on Abbot and *Avoiding the Gods*.

Fulton, Graham (1988) 'Pen was mightier than the scalpel for Perth man' In: *The Perthshire Advertiser,* 10/06/1988, p. 3. Note: in a handwritten note with this press cutting, in Acc. 11978/5 (NLS) Fulton claims this article is more an appreciation of Abbot's work than a literary/ critical review. Despite Fulton's claims, it is one of the most biographically detailed of articles on Abbot.

Lockerbie, Catherine (1988) 'Evening of Poetry and Music'. In: *The Scotsman,* 27/2/1988. Note: this is a review of Abbot's reading at the Royal Museum of Scotland, but much of the review is taken up with a discussion of one of Abbot's guest readers, Sorley MacLean.

Anon (1992) 'Ian Abbot Dedication' In: *Faultlines 1.* Inverness, p. 12.

Nicholson, Colin (1992) 'A Kind of Logic: Ian Abbot 1944-1989' In: *Poem, Purpose and Place: Shaping Identity in Contemporary Scottish Verse.* Polygon, Edinburgh, pp. 238-245.

Keay, John & Keay, Julia (eds.) (1994) 'Ian Abbot (1947-1989)' in: Collins Encyclopaedia of Scotland. HarperCollins, London, p. 1.

Hutchison, Alexander (2003) 'Remembering Ian Abbot' In: *Chapman 102-103,* pp 99-101.

McCaffery, Richie (2013) 'Ferns like poems: The poetry of Ian Abbot' in *Northwords Now 24,* p. 17.

McCaffery, Richie (2015) 'Ian Abbot (1947-1989) In: *The Next Review, Vol. 2, Issue 4,* n.p

Anon (n.d.) 'Ian Abbot (1947-1989)' In: *Gazetteer for Scotland.* Accessed online at: *http://www.scottish-places.info/people/famousfirst1889.html.*

Reviews of *Avoiding the Gods*

Anon. (1988). Review. In: *The Edinburgh Review 82,* pp. 149-151.
Bell, Robin (1988). 'Poetry'. In: *Books in Scotland 29,* pp. 21-22.
Gillies, Valerie (1988) 'Nemesis from Arcady' In: *Chapman 53,* Summer, pp. 85-87.
Gladstone, Mary & Royle, Trevor (1988) 'Tuesday Review' on *BBC Radio Scotland,* 22/03/1988.
Hutchsion, Alexander (1988) Unpublished response/review to 'Tuesday Review', accessed in Acc.12737/14, National Library of Scotland.
Hutchison, Alexander (1988). Review. In: *Radical Scotland 33,* p. 33.
McManus, Tony (1988). 'Avoiding Gods and Bending Ears' In: *Cencrastus 29,* pp. 31-32.
Nicholson, Colin (1988). Review. In: *Lines Review 107,* pp. 45-47.
Bendon, Chris (1989). Review. In: *Acumen Nine,* pp. 79-81.
Jenkins, Lucien (1989) 'Recent poetry'. In: *Skoob 1,* pp. 44-48.
Nairn, Thom (1989) Review. In: *Scottish Literary Journal Supplement. No. 30,* pp 54-57.

Index of First Lines

I – The astrologer 27
II – The knight 28
III – The Queen 29

A

A body of work 18
A cancelled poetry lesson 41
A crofter buried 17
After the Equinox 126
Agates 45
A late note from a prodigal 67
A late note to my mother 70
Along the wall the heads look down 148
A mad old woman dying 101
A.M. alphabet 136
A memoir from the mind-camp 80
An educated rabbit's view of the snare 108
An inland sea 26
A real death 112
A resurrected long dead soldier 91
Ariel 11
A search for lodgings 51
A summer engagement 117
A vanished poet's house 58
Avoiding the gods 23
A woman of my acquaintance 73

B

Before the flood 24
Bird's eye view 65
Black name 77
Blizzard conditions 43
Brain coral 66

C

Caliban rising 19
Cameraman 109
Chalybeate spring 78
Climbing through ammonites 100
Crossing Carn Donnachaidh 64
Crossing the ford 7

D

Death in the rose 156
Death watch 48
Departures 86
Digging for victory 36
Drawing to a close 42
Dreams in the evening 144
Drifts 72
Drowning among mountains 75

E

Evening 137
Ewe against the fence 21
Exile 40

F

Ferns like poems 2
Fever 55
Finishing the picture 74
Fishing through a hole 52
Forms 3

G

Ga-Cridhe 63

H

Harbingers 79
He caught me by the roadside 120
Hephaestus preaching 37
Here 83
Here in September 155
Here is where 151
History rolls away 152
How I forgot 118
How important 84

I

I know that somewhere 153
In my veins the pack is running 162
Inside the altarpiece 8
I seem 123

K

Keeper and cottage 98
Khamsin 134

L

Lament of the horse-bit 49
Landscape of a Highland gentleman 32
Landscapes 114
Last dip of the year 57
Laurel bush 50
Life history 104
Lifeline 60
Looking for wild men 105
Looking with new eyes 97
Love in February 93

M

Marriages 12
Monster 61
Montezuma 5
Moths at the window 96
Musteline 111
Mykonos 135

N

November 94

O

Omens 132, 161
On certain nights 110
One place in the Highlands 31
On that day 87

P

Passing through September 103
Plain of jars 138
Prayer to the god of the mine 142
Promenaders on the tideline 35

Q

Quiet evenings at home 46

R

Raptor 127
Retrospective premonitions 146
Returning 139
rights iv
Rites of passage 68
River of deep winter, when the ice 150

S

Scott's first voyage 13
Shrapnel 30
Sloughing 54
Small hours 88
Speaking in solitary 102
Spoor 10
Spring Equinox 95
Stalactites 92
Starlings 116

T

The beetle man 34
The bestiary of Cortes 4
The comforting word 99
The last entry of a polar explorer 16
The magi in solitude 140
The mechanisms of the gin 71
The mine 85
The omnibus 115
The oriental archer 44
The poetry of television 113
The retired soldier's lesson 129
The sailor's widow embroidering 47
The shadow-wolf 62
The suicides of April 25
The wind blows 161
Thoughts after the funeral, for W. 143
Three words, no more 154
Throughout the green night 119
Tick 33
To Hilary 124
Trees 160
Tumour 131

U

Uninvited guests 76

V

Vestal 6

W

Ward seven – December 39
Wax resist 56
Within me 149
Writing late 145

Y

You will say 159